Essential Documents
for Saving Tax

THE COMPLEMENTARY WEBSITE

The http://books.indicator.co.uk website gives you instant access to all the ready-to-use documents, tools, policies, etc. that complement this publication.

Go to

http://books.indicator.co.uk

and enter your access code
VCT883

THE CD-ROM

Don't have access to the Internet?
Call Customer Services on 01233 653500 to request a CD-ROM.

Indicator has joined forces with **FL Memo**

Introduction

Tax is a difficult subject to deal with at the best of times. To make matters worse, the tendency to label everything "tax avoidance" means that it is now even more essential to have the correct paperwork in place to defend your position. The Taxman won't let you claim that a particular tax exemption applies or that your intentions were other than tax avoidance if you don't have the paperwork to prove it. Paperwork is essential in keeping the Taxman off your back. Should you find yourself on the end of a routine enquiry, it's a safe bet that the first thing he will want to see is your paperwork. And although the Taxman may start his initial enquiries into your current year returns, he can then go back over the last four years of returns and records. So getting the paperwork right now will stand you in good stead for the future.

For this reason, we decided to produce Essential Documents for Saving Tax. It includes over 140 letters, policies, checklists and tools which cover all areas of taxation. It is divided into eleven chapters which cover everything from company cars to VAT. Each chapter is accompanied by a useful commentary which describes how and when each document should be used. And with the complementary Download Zone website you can copy or adapt and print each one to suit your needs.

Ideally this book should become a useful companion and help you stay one step ahead of the Taxman. If you would like to see other documents added, please contact us and we will endeavour to include them in future editions.

Tony Court
Editor in Chief

Table of contents

Section 1- Cars

Section 2 - CGT

Section 3 - Dealing with tax investigations

Section 4 - Elections and claims

Section 5 - Employee benefits and expenses

Section 6 - Employee remuneration

Section 7 - IHT

Section 8 - Profit extraction

Section 9 - Property investment

Section 10 - Status

Section 11 - VAT

Section 1

Cars

Business mileage record

Employees and directors are required to keep a detailed record of journeys for which they receive a mileage allowance from their employer or where they claim a tax deduction for business travel. A copy of the records should be retained by the employer and by the individual, as HMRC may ask to see them.

OWN CARS

Employers can pay directors and employees tax and NI-free allowances for business mileage at rates shown in the table below. These are known as approved mileage allowance payments.

Where the sum paid by the employer is less than the tax and NI-free amount, the director or employee is entitled to claim a tax deduction for the difference.

DIRECTOR/EMPLOYEE OWNED CAR	TAX-FREE AMOUNT	NI-FREE AMOUNT
First 10,000 miles of business travel per tax year	45p	45p
Subsequent business travel	25p	45p
Allowance for taking passenger on business journey	5p	5p

COMPANY CARS

An employer may also reimburse a director or employee for the cost of fuel for business journeys travelled in a company car. The payments can be made tax and NI free. HMRC publishes recommended mileage rates for reimbursement, which are updated quarterly. These are referred to as advisory fuel rates. You can find the current rates by visiting: http://www.hmrc.gov.uk/cars/advisory_fuel_current.htm.

BUSINESS MILEAGE RECORD

Name: _____   Month/year: _____

Date	Reason for journey	to	from	Miles	Pence per mile	Claim
Mileage allowance claimed from last 6 April ignoring this claim						
						£0,00
						£0,00
						£0,00
						£0,00
						£0,00
						£0,00
						£0,00
						£0,00
						£0,00
						£0,00
						£0,00
						£0,00
						£0,00
						£0,00
Total mileage and amount for this claim				-		**£0,00**
Business mileage carried forward for tax year to date						

1. Where travel was in a personally-owned car and total s no more than 10,000 miles since last 5 April the tax and NI-free mileage rate is the maximum of 45p.
2. Where travel was in a personally-owned car and total s more than 10,000 miles since last 5 April the tax and NI-free mileage rate is the maximum of 25p.
3. Where the travel was in a company car HMRC publ shes a suggested tax and NI-free mileage rate, which it updates each quarter (see http://www.hmrc.gov.uk/cars/advisory_fuel_current.htm)
4. Record only travel that is undertaken for business purposes. That excludes travel between your home and your normal place of work.

Cars and car allowances policy

You only need a policy statement on company cars or car allowances if you actually provide your employees with them. If only a couple of employees have company cars, you might find it easier to include the provision in their contracts of employment rather than in a staff handbook that applies to everyone. It's still worth including the provisions on driving and mobile phones for everyone.

A COMPANY CAR

When providing an employee with a company car, you need to think carefully about who is going to pay for what in terms of fuel, insurance, MOT, licensing, repairs, etc., who can drive the car, to what extent it can be used for personal purposes or taken abroad, what obligations you are going to place on the employee in relation to looking after it properly, reporting defects, accidents or parking/ speeding fines and in what circumstances you can ask for the car back, etc. Our **Cars and Car Allowances Policy** statement covers all these issues and many more. Where the car is provided for the employee's personal use as well as for business use, note that it cannot be withdrawn during any period of notice, garden leave or maternity leave, unless an allowance in lieu of the benefit of the car is provided instead. If you do withdraw it, that represents a breach of contract.

THE COST OF REPAIRS

Car repairs don't come cheap, so you will want to ensure the employee pays for them in the event that they cause damage to the vehicle due to their negligence or wilful default. Where there's an accident, you might also want the employee to pay the insurance excess. Our policy statement provides for the employee to bear the cost in these circumstances. However, you will also need to ensure that a signed deductions clause appears in the employee's contract of employment to allow deductions to be made from their salary to cover the relevant costs. It's only possible to have the deductions clause in the policy statement if it clearly forms part of the employee's contract of employment. If this is the case, just amend our statement accordingly.

UPWARDLY MOBILE

Whilst it's not normally your problem if an employee gets in trouble with the police for using their

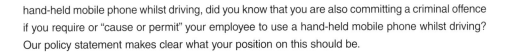

hand-held mobile phone whilst driving, did you know that you are also committing a criminal offence if you require or "cause or permit" your employee to use a hand-held mobile phone whilst driving? Our policy statement makes clear what your position on this should be.

VEHICLE TRACKING

Finally, our policy includes an optional section on vehicle tracking which you should include if you intend to fit satellite tracking systems to company cars. If you do this, you should only monitor the car during business use and there should be a privacy button installed to enable the monitoring to be disabled during private use. Vehicle tracking is covered by the **Data Protection Act 1998** and therefore you should first carry out an impact assessment to consider whether the benefits justify the adverse impact on employees.

CARS AND CAR ALLOWANCES POLICY

Company cars

Subject to holding a current, full driving licence, some employees are provided with a car for use in the performance of their job duties. If you are provided with a company car, this will be set out in your contract of employment. Unless you are notified otherwise, a company car may be used for both business and private use, subject to such restrictions and upon such conditions (if any) as the Company may from time to time impose. In particular, the employee is the only person authorised to drive the car. Under no circumstances may any other person drive the car.

The company car may not be used for:

- any business purposes other than those undertaken on behalf of the Company
- hire or reward (either goods or passengers)
- racing, pace making, rally driving or any other competitive event
- towing.

Employees are only provided with company cars at the absolute discretion of the Company and it may change its rules and procedures on company cars at any time and from time to time.

The Company reserves the right to set a maximum lease value on company cars and/or to specify the make, model and colour that will be provided.

The Company will pay for the MOT, licensing, insurance, maintenance, repair and servicing of company cars (provided repairs and service are not caused by the employee's negligence or wilful default) and when necessary replacement thereof. However, employees have no contractual right to a replacement car. The Company will also pay for the cost of petrol/diesel (as appropriate) for business use only. The employee must pay for petrol/diesel for all private mileage. When any manufacturer's cover expires, the Company will also arrange to provide and pay for emergency breakdown/roadside assistance cover through a motoring organisation selected by the Company.

The employee will be responsible for any income tax and National Insurance liability as assessed by HM Revenue & Customs in respect of the use of the car.

The employee must not permit the car to be taken out of Great Britain without the prior consent of their line manager.

The Company will retain all documents relating to the registration of the car. However, the employee is responsible for ensuring the car has a valid MOT certificate and a valid licence (tax) disc and for ensuring the car is properly maintained and serviced. As stated above, the Company will generally bear the cost of these matters. Appointments for MOT testing and servicing must be made with a garage approved in advance by the Company. Employees are required to identify the service dates in line with the vehicle log book and mileage record.

The employee is also responsible for ensuring the car is properly looked after at all times and is responsible for the cleanliness of it, together with its equipment and fittings. The employee must ensure that it is kept in a roadworthy condition, that regular checks are made of tyre tread, tyre pressure, lights, brakes, oil, water coolant, fuel, screen wash and battery and that it conforms with current road traffic legislation and that the provisions and conditions of the policy of insurance relating thereto are observed and that such policy is not rendered void or voidable. The Company may seek to recoup any losses in the event of damage caused to the car by the employee's negligence or wilful default. In addition, the employee is responsible for the excess which is required to be paid which is not recoverable from the insurance company should the vehicle be involved in an accident, irrespective of the responsibility for the accident. The employee accepts that the Company shall be entitled to deduct the cost of repair of any such damage and/or the cost of the insurance excess from his or her wages and, if this applies, a relevant deduction from wages clause will be set out in the employee's contract of employment.

Employees are not permitted to carry out any alterations to the car, nor are they permitted to fit car radios, stereo equipment, fog lamps, roof racks, tow bars or any other accessories.

Personal items are left in the car entirely at the employee's own risk and the Company does not accept any liability for loss, theft or damage of personal items.

The employee must report to the Company forthwith:

- vehicle defects or damage to the car
- any theft or loss of the car
- any road traffic accident in which the employee may be involved whilst driving the car, whether or not that occurred on the Company's business
- any fixed penalty notice or any order of any court to endorse the employee's driving licence or to disqualify him or her from holding a driving licence, whether or not that consequence occurred whilst driving on the Company's business
- any other event which results in the employee being ineligible to drive the car.

The employee must also immediately report any theft or loss of the car or reportable road traffic accident involving the car to the police.

Where a road traffic accident also involves a third party's vehicle, the employee is responsible for obtaining the registration number of that vehicle and the particulars of any persons involved in the accident, as well as the names and addresses of any witnesses to the accident.

The employee must drive within the law and abide by all requirements of road traffic law and the Highway Code, including but not limited to:

- ensuring that a valid tax disc is displayed in the windscreen of the car
- ensuring that traffic signs and speed limits are observed
- ensuring that the car is properly parked and not in breach of any road traffic regulations.

The employee is responsible for the payment of any and all fines incurred as a result of a motoring offence whilst the car is in the employee's possession, including parking and speeding fines and, if this applies, the employee accepts that the Company shall be entitled to deduct the cost of any such fines from the employee's wages and a relevant deductions from wages clause will be set out in the employee's contract of employment.

Upon request, the employee must provide his or her full driving licence for inspection.

Failure to observe these rules or failure to use the car in a reasonable and responsible manner may result in the Company withdrawing the use of the car from the employee concerned. In addition, a failure to observe these rules will be regarded as a disciplinary offence and will be dealt with in accordance with the Company's disciplinary procedure. Depending on the seriousness of the breach, it may constitute potential gross misconduct rendering the employee liable to summary dismissal.

In the event that the Company suspends the employee from the performance of his or her duties in accordance with the Company's disciplinary procedure, the employee will not be entitled to the continued use of the car during that period of suspension.

The employee must promptly return or account for the car and deliver up the keys to .... *(insert name of contact)* in the following circumstances:

- on the termination of the employee's employment
- if, for whatever reason, the employee ceases to hold a valid and current licence to drive private motor cars
- during any period of extended leave granted by the Company
- if the employee is convicted of a careless, reckless or dangerous driving offence, at the discretion of the Company
- if the car is involved in an excessive number of accidents whilst being used by the employee, as determined by the Company
- if the employee violates the terms of this policy or fails to use the car in a reasonable and responsible manner, as determined by the Company
- if there is an unacceptable increase in the insurance premium for the car as a result of the number of penalty points endorsed on the employee's driving licence, as determined by the Company.

If one of these applies, the employee accepts that his or her failure to return or account for the car will entitle the Company to withhold any outstanding monies/wages due from the Company to the employee up to the value of the car and a relevant deduction from wages clause to this effect will be set out in the employee's contract of employment.

Contributions to private use

Where the company requires the employee to contribute to the running costs of the car for purposes other than company business, payments are due no later than the last day of the month to which the contribution relates. A contribution received late, that is, after the end of the month for which it was due, will count as a contribution for the month in which it is paid.

Car allowances

In lieu of the provision of a company car, the employee may elect by notice in writing to the Company to receive a monthly car allowance of such amount as shall be notified by the Company from time to time. This allowance shall be added to and paid on the due date for payment of salary.

Driving and mobile phones

Some employees are required to drive on the Company's business as part of their job duties. Operating a mobile phone whilst driving reduces concentration and increases the likelihood of an accident. It is also a criminal offence in certain circumstances. This section therefore also sets out the Company's requirements in relation to employees using mobile phones whilst driving on Company business.

It applies irrespective of whether the employee uses a Company-provided mobile phone or their own personal mobile phone and irrespective of whether they are driving a company car or their own car.

Employees are completely prohibited from using a hand-held mobile phone or similar hand-held electronic device whilst driving as part of their job duties, whether this is to make or receive telephone calls, send or read text or image/picture messages, send or receive facsimiles or to access the Internet or e-mail. If any employee is discovered contravening this rule, they will face serious action under the Company's disciplinary procedure. In view of the potential health and safety implications, it may also constitute gross misconduct and could render the employee liable to summary dismissal. If an employee does wish to use a hand-held mobile phone when driving, he or she must stop the car and completely turn off the car's engine before using the mobile phone. A person is regarded as "driving" for the purposes of the law if the engine is running, even if their vehicle is stationary. This means employees must not use a hand-held phone at traffic lights, during traffic jams or at other times when the engine is still running.

A hands-free phone is one that does not require the user to hold it at any point during the course of its operation. A mobile phone that is attached to fixed speakers and does not require the user to hold it whilst in use (for example, because it is stored in a cradle) would be covered, as would a hands-free mobile phone with voice activation. If the phone needs to be held in the user's hand at some point during its operation, for example to dial the number or to end the call, it is not hands-free. If employees are required to drive as part of their job duties and they wish to use a mobile phone, they must ensure they have the appropriate hands-free equipment for the phone. However, even with hands-free equipment, driving and conducting a telephone conversation are both demanding tasks and the employee should take all reasonable steps to ensure they do not carry out these tasks at the same time. The employee should therefore make use of any voicemail or call divert facility available, rather than make or receive "live" calls. The employee should then stop regularly in safe places to check for voicemail messages and to make and return calls. If an employee does need to make or receive a call whilst driving on Company business and he or she has the appropriate hands-free equipment, these calls should nevertheless be limited to essential calls and only when it is safe to do so.

[Vehicle tracking

The Company reserves the right to install monitoring devices such as satellite tracking systems in all company cars to track the movement of the vehicle during business use. Such devices may record or transmit information such as the location of the car, the distance it has covered, its speed and related information about the user's driving habits. An employee will be advised if a monitoring device has been installed, or will be installed, in their company car and will also be advised of the nature of the monitoring that will take place.

As company cars may also be used for private use, the Company does not wish to monitor the car when used privately. Therefore, where a monitoring device has been installed, a "privacy button" or similar arrangement will be provided to enable the monitoring to be disabled or deactivated by the employee during private use. Monitoring must not, however, be disabled at any time during business use. If any employee is discovered contravening this rule, they will face serious action under the Company's disciplinary procedure.

The purposes of vehicle tracking are to:

- ensure drivers are not in breach of the Working Time Regulations 1998
- help prevent accidents by monitoring driver speed and habits
- maximise driver performance and productivity and improve customer service
- improve fuel economy by monitoring and managing company cars more effectively
- protect the health, safety and welfare of lone drivers by ensuring they can be more easily located in the event of an emergency.

In some cases, the Company may be under a legal obligation to monitor the use of vehicles, even if used privately, for example by fitting a tachograph as a permanent fixture in a lorry. In these cases, the Company's legal obligation will always take precedence and the monitoring cannot be turned off.

The Company may use the information obtained from vehicle monitoring in any subsequent disciplinary action where the data shows there has been a breach by the employee of Company rules and procedures.]

Lump sum contribution agreement

If the employee pays an amount towards the purchase price of a company car, it's good practice to write this into the company car agreement as it provides evidence that the payment relates to provision of the car.

CAPITAL CONTRIBUTION

A capital contribution can be made by a director or employee towards the cost of either the car itself or any of the accessories which are taken into account in determining its price for taxable benefit purposes. The capital contribution is deducted from the list price of the car when calculating the taxable benefit.

Example. If the car attracts a tax charge of 24% per year, then making a capital contribution of £5,000 will save them tax on £1,200 (£5,000 x 24%) p.a. If they are a higher rate taxpayer, they would save £480 p.a. (40% x £1,200). If they are an additional rate taxpayer, they will save £540 (45% x £1,200) p.a.

MAXIMUM CONTRIBUTION

There is a ceiling of £5,000 on the amount of any capital contribution which may be taken into account for these purposes.

ON OR BEFORE PROVISION OF THE CAR

HMRC expects the payment to be made on or before the provision of the car or it may try to argue that a later payment relates to a contribution towards private use instead, which means it will only be set against the taxable benefit in the year the payment is made and not subsequent years.

CONTRIBUTION AGREEMENT

So while there's no requirement for the lump sum contribution to be written into the company car agreement, it's good practice to make it contractual as this provides evidence that the payment relates to provision of the car.

WHAT HAPPENS WHEN THE CAR IS SOLD/EXCHANGED?

The money the employee has paid should be refundable after their share of the depreciation in market value since purchase has been taken into account.

LUMP SUM CONTRIBUTION AGREEMENT

Agreement concerning a capital contribution towards the purchase of Company car registration
……….…..... *(insert registration number)* (the "Car") to be provided by ……….……..... *(insert company name)* (the "Company") for private use by …………………………….... *(insert name)* (the "Director/Employee").

The Employee agrees to make a capital contribution of ..... *(insert figure*)* towards the purchase of the Car, to be paid by the employee within 30 days of the Car being purchased by the Company.

Upon sale of the Car, the Employee will be entitled to a refund of said capital contribution, but only after the Employee's share of depreciation in market value since purchase has been taken into account.

Agreement
As a condition of the Car being available, I agree to make the payment referred to above and accept a deduction for depreciation from any refund due to me when the Car is sold.

Signed...

Date ....

* maximum of £5,000.

Memo: invoices for motor expenses

How expenses are controlled is always at the top of HMRC's list of questions during a compliance visit. Using our memo should help you to dismiss enquiries about motor expenses very quickly, before they become too detailed.

COMPLIANCE VISIT

A compliance visit is often referred to as a PAYE visit, i.e. an inspection of your books and records centred around your payroll but specifically trying to unearth, as yet, untaxed payments and benefits in kind. The inspectors will ask for a full list of the current balances on your nominal ledger, and then for an analysis of what has been posted to accounts, such as cleaning, repairs, motor expenses, entertainment, etc. They are looking for hidden payments to, or benefits for, employees. This is where having a computerised accounts system can come in handy and you can simply print out what's in there. They will also trust you to get any invoices they are interested in looking at.

COVER YOURSELF

As a rule of thumb, every invoice relating to a company car needs to be in the name of the employer for it to receive a tax deduction for the expense. It will save problems later if you make this issue clear to employees, you can use our **Memo: Invoices for Motor Expenses** for this purpose. Following this up with a review of all motor expenses invoices over, say, £300 should limit your tax exposure to this sort of error. If you do find a mistake, send a copy of the invoice back to the supplier and ask for one in the company's name.

MEMO: INVOICES FOR MOTOR EXPENSES

To: all employees with company cars

It has come to the Company's attention that certain motor expenses claims have been submitted without the appropriate documentation being attached. In order for the Company to recover these costs for tax purposes and to avoid Company car drivers being taxed on a separate benefit in kind please take note that:

1. Invoices for repairs and maintenance

The Company will pay for the MOT, licensing, insurance, maintenance, repair and servicing of Company cars. However, the contract/invoice for said maintenance, repair and servicing **must** be in the name of the Company, not the Company car driver.

2. Accessories

If a vehicle is used for business purposes, VAT on repairs and maintenance can be recovered provided the work done is paid for by the Company. However, VAT charged on accessories fitted to a car when it is purchased cannot be reclaimed, even if separately itemised on the sales invoice. VAT can be reclaimed on accessories subsequently purchased and fitted to a vehicle for business reasons, provided the accessory remains part of the vehicle.

....*(insert signature of MD or FD)*

....*(insert date)*

Pool car journey record

In order to apply for pool car status you will need to provide HMRC with evidence of how the car is used. So you'll need to keep a record of all the journeys undertaken to show that the car satisifies the strict pool car conditions.

PROOF OF JOURNEY

To satisfy HMRC that a vehicle is a genuine pool car, you need to have evidence that the car has not been used by one director/employee to the exclusion of others and that there was no non-incidental private use. Using our **Pool Car Journey Record** is an excellent way of proving when the car was used, who used it and why.

This will provide proof that there has been no private use of the vehicle (except for the rare occasion when it forms part of a business journey; for example, to keep an early appointment the employee takes the car home the night before).

Keep the record in the glove compartment of the car for the duration of the month, so there can be no excuses about failure to complete it. However, do ensure that the form is filed away at the end of the month. Make sure the records are kept safely - even after pool car status is confirmed the journey records are likely to be checked by HMRC during an employer compliance visit.

POOL CAR JOURNEY RECORD

For the month of ....*(insert month)*

Pool car...*(insert make, model and registration of car)*

Driver	Date	Journey(s)		Notes
		From	**To**	

Pool car policy

Banning private use is essential for a car to be considered a pool car by HMRC. A verbal ban may work but it's far more sensible to have a policy written into the employee's contract. This will also help convince an inspector that you operate a genuine pool car arrangement.

TERMS OF USE

Verbally banning employees from using pool cars for private journeys was good enough for one VAT tribunal; however, we recommend that you'll be on much safer ground by introducing a **Pool Car Policy**. Always make your intentions clear from the start of a pool car arrangement by explicitly banning private journeys. This way when buying your next pool car you should be able to claim back the VAT on it.

This policy lays out the terms of use for pool cars: that private use is banned, all journeys are to be logged on the pool car journey record, and that the car should not be kept at or near someone's house except in exceptional circumstances.

The policy also makes it clear that each car is not for the exclusive use of one particular person; this is vitally important in establishing its pool car status. The car must be driven only by authorised personnel and you must obtain a copy of their driving licence before you allow them to drive it. All fuel must be paid for by the company.

There is also a clause relating to damage to the vehicle. By signing the employment contract, the employee is agreeing to repay the company should the car be damaged due to the employee's negligence or wilful neglect. They will also accept responsibility for an excess payment should the car be involved in an accident, regardless of the circumstances.

Together with the journey record, by including this policy in your employee's contract it should help to convince an inspector that you operate a genuine pool car arrangement.

POOL CAR POLICY

A pool car can be made available (but not exclusively) to some employees for use in the performance of their duties subject to them holding a current, full driving licence. A pool car must only be used for business journeys, the car must be kept overnight at the Company's premises, and is subject to any other such restrictions and upon such conditions (if any) as the Company may from time to time impose. In particular, only authorised employees can drive the pool car. Under no circumstances may any other person drive the car. The cost of petrol/diesel (as appropriate) in running the pool car is paid for by the Company.

Employees are only provided with a pool car at the discretion of the Company and it may change its rules and procedures on pool cars at any time and from time to time.

If, occasionally, an employee takes a car home so as to make an early start on a business journey the following morning, it is Company policy to allow this only where starting the journey from the company's premises would have caused unreasonable delay.

An employee staying away from home overnight because of a business trip may use the car to go out for a meal in the evening.

The Company may seek to recoup any losses in the event of damage caused to the car by the employee's negligence or wilful neglect. In addition, the employee is responsible for the excess which is required to be paid which is not recoverable from the insurance company should the vehicle be involved in an accident, irrespective of the responsibility for the accident. By signing their contract of employment, the employee accepts that the Company shall be entitled to deduct the cost of repair of any such damage and/or the cost of the insurance excess from the employee's wages.

Personal items are left in the car entirely at the employee's own risk and the Company does not accept any liability for loss, theft or damage of personal items.

The employee must report to the Company forthwith: vehicle defects, any road traffic accident, any fixed penalty notice or any order of any court to endorse the employee's driving licence or to disqualify them from holding a driving licence, whether or not that consequence occurred whilst driving on Company business, and any other event which results in the employee being ineligible to drive the car.

Upon request, the employee must provide their full driving licence for inspection.

Failure to observe these rules will be regarded as a disciplinary offence and will be dealt with in accordance with the Company's disciplinary procedure. Depending on the seriousness of the breach, it may constitute gross misconduct rendering the employee liable to summary dismissal.

Pool car status letter

A pool car can be very tax efficient but in order to get one past HMRC you'll need to meet some strict conditions. To avoid uncertainty, use this letter to compile all your evidence and obtain HMRC's approval.

NO PRIVATE USE

Get a pool car past HMRC and you can secure some excellent tax savings - no taxable benefit on the driver, no fuel benefit charge and no employers' NI. But to obtain this status, you'll need to gather evidence together about the use of the pool car.

STRICT CONDITIONS

The conditions that have to be met are: **(1)** it must be available to and actually used by more than one employee; **(2)** it must not be used by one employee to the exclusion of others; **(3)** it should not normally be kept overnight at an employee's home; and **(4)** it must not be used for private journeys except as a small part of a business journey. Given that the rules provide a total exemption from any tax charge, it's not surprising that HMRC applies them very strictly.

CONFIRMATION

Use our **Pool Car Status Letter** to work through what HMRC is after. Send it in with copies of the employees' driving licences and the **Pool Car Journey Record**. The decision about whether the vehicle will be accepted as a pool car will normally be taken by HMRC (at inspector level), although an appeal may be made on the issue to the First-tier Tribunal.

POOL CAR STATUS LETTER

HMRC
………………………….   *(insert address)*
………………………….

………………………….

Your ref: ……………….   *(insert employer's PAYE reference)*

………………………….   *(insert date)*

Dear ………………………….   *(insert name)*

RE: Pool car status

The purpose of this letter is to seek confirmation that we are correctly treating certain company vehicles as pool cars. In support of this assertion we make the following points and have enclosed supporting evidence.

The car is available to and used by more than one employee

Everyone who needs to make business trips uses the vehicle(s). Attached are:

1. Photocopies of driving licences of all employee drivers.

2. A copy of a journey record for the month of …. *(insert month)* for each pool car. This representative period clearly shows that the vehicles in question are used by more than one employee.

3. Copies of letters to the Company's insurance broker notifying them of the people using the vehicle, plus their reply notifying us of the increase in premium.

Any private use is incidental to its business use

There is of course a de-minimus private use with any pool vehicle but ours is small in extent and infrequent representing as it does, on average, no more than 5% of the vehicle's annual mileage. For example, an employee staying away from home overnight because of a business trip may use the car to go out for a meal in the evening because this is merely incidental to the main business journey.

Kept overnight on the business premises

Occasionally an employee takes a car home so as to make an early start on a business journey the following morning. It is Company policy to allow this only where starting the journey form the company's premises would have caused unreasonable delay. A copy of the Company Pool Car Policy is attached.

The total number of nights on which the pool car was taken home for this reason in the (representative period studied by the Company) was [..... *(insert percentage)* %] which is considerably less than the 60% nights of the year (or period) rule of thumb we understand you normally accept.

Yours sincerely

…………………….. *(insert signature)*

Private fuel agreement

If an employer pays for even £1 of fuel for a private journey in a company car, the full tax charge for car fuel hits. To avoid the charge, have an agreement in place to require the director or employee to reimburse the full cost of providing private fuel.

FUEL BENEFIT CHARGE

In addition to the company car benefit, a director or employee who is provided with a company car may be liable to a fuel benefit charge. This fuel benefit will arise on any free or subsidised fuel provided for private journeys.

HOW MUCH IS IT?

When a company pays for fuel used in private journeys whether for a single journey or mulitple (e.g. five or 50,000 miles), the tax charge remains the same. The fuel benefit is calculated by taking the percentage used to calculate the car benefit and multiplying it by a set figure for the tax year, The set figure for fuel benefit for cars is £21,700 for 2014/15. Depending on the company car's CO_2 emissions, the annual tax bill for the employee could be over £3,000 with the employer having to pay up to over £1,000 in the corresponding Class 1A NI bill.

AVOIDING THE CHARGE

To avoid the fuel benefit charge, employees must show that the company doesn't meet the cost of any fuel for these private journeys. There are two ways to do this:

- the employee pays for all fuel and only claims for the business miles driven at HMRC's advisory fuel rates
- the company pays for all fuel (usually via a fuel card) and the employee reimburses the company for the cost of fuel used for private journeys using HMRC's advisory fuel rates.

Must be a requirement

It's not enough for the employee to simply reimburse the cost of the private fuel; the law says to escape the tax and NI bill, employees must be "required" to do so. HMRC accepts that the requirement to reimburse the cost of private mileage exists where the company has a policy to this effect and makes this clear to its company car drivers. Use our **Private Fuel Agreement** to document this requirement.

Note. If the employee only makes a partial reimbursement, this will not reduce the fuel benefit - the employee must reimburse the full cost.

PRIVATE FUEL AGREEMENT

Agreement concerning fuel for use in company car .... *(insert registration number)* provided by the Company for ....*(insert name of the director/employee).*

The Company will pay for the cost of petrol/diesel (as appropriate) for business use of your company car. You will pay for petrol/diesel for all private mileage.

If the Company inadvertently pays for petrol/diesel for your private mileage during a tax year (6 April to 5 April), you will reimburse the Company for this (at HMRC's advisory fuel rate).

For example, the Company pays you for the cost of fuel for a journey, which later turns out to have not been genuine business mileage. You are then required to make good the cost of that fuel. Ideally this payment will be made within the tax year but must be made without unreasonable delay.

Agreement

I agree to make the payment referred to above if the Company inadvertently pays for my private fuel.

Signed: ………………………….

Date: ………………………….

Top-up payments agreement

If an employee or director makes a monthly contribution towards their company car, this can reduce the taxable benefit providing it can be shown that the contribution is required and is in respect of private use of the car.

MONTHLY COMPANY CAR CONTRIBUTIONS

It's common practice under many company car schemes for employees to have to make monthly contributions to their employer for use of the car. Providing the agreement is structured correctly, these contributions can reduce the taxable company car benefit, saving the employee tax and the company Class 1A NI.

Required. The law states that the employee must be required to make a contribution which suggests that it must be a contractual obligation, otherwise no deduction will be allowed. Use our **Top-up Payments Agreement** to document this requirement.

Note. The contribution must be in respect of private use of the car, and not merely to secure a better car than would otherwise have been available, in which case no deduction would apply.

TOP-UP PAYMENTS AGREEMENT

Agreement concerning use of the company car registration ……….... *(insert registration number)* (the "Car") provided by ...…….....*(insert company name)* (the "Company") for private use by …………....*(insert name)* (the "Director/Employee").

Until further notice, the Company is making the Car available to the Employee for their private use, subject to the Employee making a payment to the Company for that private use. The payment will be ......*(insert figure*)* per month or such other amount as the Company may, in its discretion, advise in writing and will be deducted from the Employee's net monthly pay.

As a condition of the Car being available for private use, I agree to make the payment referred to above for that use.

Signed: ………………………….

Date: ………………………….

---

*   This could be either a fixed amount or an amount calculated by a formula. The following are examples of the wording that could be used:
   (a) £100; or
   (b) the figure calculated as 20% of the leasing cost of the car for the previous month; or
   (c) the figure calculated as 20p per private mile in excess of 750 private miles driven in the previous month.

Use of van agreement

If your company makes a van available for private use then there is a benefit in kind. This charge comes into play when private use exceeds normal business commuting.

COMPANY VAN BENEFIT

There is a fixed taxable benefit charge of £3,000 a year for private use of a van (with a laden weight of 3.5 tonnes or less). And another £550 for free or subsidised fuel for private use. However, these charges come into play when private use exceeds normal commuting.

To avoid the charge, you should make it a condition of the driver's employment that whilst they can use the van for ordinary commuting, no other private use (i.e. any non-business journey excluding commuting) is permitted by them (or their family) unless they pay for it. Our **Use of Van Agreement** can be used to document this.

Note. HMRC is likely to accept that the van is only used for ordinary commuting if the employee has the use of an alternative vehicle for private journeys. If they have no access to another vehicle, HMRC may question the private use, so make a note of the situation in your records.

"Insignificant" use is permitted without triggering the benefit, for example, using the van in an emergency or for an occasional short journey. If any of your drivers fit into the insignificant private use category there should be no charge and nothing to declare on your Form P11D for the tax year.

USE OF VAN AGREEMENT

Agreement concerning use of company van registration ……………......*(insert registration number)* (the "Van") provided by ......*(insert company name)* (the "Company") to ………... *(insert name)* (the "Director"/"Employee"), NI number …………... *(insert NI number)*.

The Van is made available to the Employee for travel on Company business. The Employee is permitted to use the Van for ordinary commuting to and from home, the Employee's place of work, but all other private use is strictly prohibited. According to HMRC guidance, prohibited private use includes using the van to do the supermarket shopping each week, taking the van away on a week's holiday or using the van outside of work for social activities.

The Employee is also required to keep a daily mileage log in the vehicle recording the reason for the journey and the number of business miles travelled.

Agreement

As a condition of the Van being provided to me, I confirm that it will not be used for any private purpose except ordinary commuting between my home and place of work.

Signed: ....

Date: ....

Section 2

CGT

Calculation of CGT pro forma

Use our calculation of capital gains tax (CGT) pro forma to quickly calculate the possible liability you have for CGT against any assets you have disposed of, or are thinking of disposing of.

CAPITAL GAINS TAX

When you sell your assets you might have to pay CGT on any profit you make. But there are loads of legal deductions that can reduce the taxable gain.

The gain is usually calculated by taking the actual disposal proceeds and deducting the purchase cost. Remember to deduct all the costs of sale and purchase, including broker's/agent's fees. Keep all this information with your tax papers.

Use our **Calculation of CGT Pro Forma** to estimate your capital gain.

Note. The rate of tax charged depends on the rate charged on the highest part of your income and whether any basic rate band is unused:

- income and gain all within basic rate   = 18% on gain
- income and gain basic rate partly unused on income   = 18% on gain to higher rate threshold

           = 28% on remainder
- income and gain above higher rate threshold   = 28% on gain.

CALCULATION OF CAPITAL GAINS TAX PRO FORMA

▶ **Fill in the red cells**

Description of asset:

Date on which asset was disposed of: | **05.04.2015**

Disposal proceeds or maket value | **£0,00**
Less:
Costs of sale | **£0,00**
| | £0,00

Net proceeds | **£0,00**

Less:
Purchase cost or value at 31 March 1982 | **£0,00**
Enhancement expenditure, e.g. property improvement costs | **£0,00**
Total | | £0,00

Less:
Specific exemptions and reliefs | **£0,00**
| | £0,00

Capital gain or loss made on asset | **£0,00**

Total of all capital gains or losses for year | **£0,00**

Less:
Annual exemption (2014/15) | £11.000,00
| | £11.000,00

Capital gains after deducting annual exemption | | £0,00

Less :
Capital losses brought forward | £0,00
| | £0,00

Taxable gain | **£0,00**
Losses carried forward to later years | £0,00

Calculation of goodwill pro forma

When you transfer a business to a limited company, you need to calculate the value of the goodwill in it. If HMRC doesn't agree with your valuation, the difference between its (lower) and your (higher) valuation will be taxed on you. A document showing how you arrived at the calculation of goodwill which also includes a price adjuster clause should help to avoid this potential tax problem.

INCORPORATING A BUSINESS

You may have started as a sole trader or a partnership but have now decided to incorporate your business. When you transfer a business to a limited company you need to calculate the value of the goodwill in it. The larger the goodwill figure, the more money you can take out of the company tax free. As you are gifting business assets, you can claim gift relief on the transfer and therefore defer any CGT liability on the gain. Use our **Calculation of Goodwill Pro Forma** to estimate the value of goodwill in your business.

PRICE ADJUSTER CLAUSE

You should also include a price adjuster clause in your valuation so that the figure can be automatically varied if HMRC doesn't agree with the valuation. This will avoid the possible problem of any difference between its (lower) and your (higher) valuation being treated as taxable, as a distribution which could result in a tax charge of either 25% of the amount overpaid for higher rate taxpayers or 30.56% for additional rate taxpayers. With a price adjuster clause, if the goodwill value is challenged by HMRC, the difference between its valuation and the original one is treated as a reduction in your director's loan account balance, therefore eliminating the tax charge.

It's best to ask HMRC to agree your valuation (in advance of submitting your tax return) by completing Form CG34 (http://www.hmrc.gov.uk/forms/cg34.pdf).

CALCULATION OF GOODWILL PRO FORMA

Name

Business name

Calculation of goodwill as at (DD/MM/YYYY)

£   £

Profit history (sole trader or partnership)

Year ended (DD/MM/YYYY)

Year ended (DD/MM/YYYY)

Year ended (DD/MM/YYYY)

-

Average annual profit (last three years)

-

Profit projection (Company)

Estimated projected maintainable profits

Yield on capital investment

Net assets transferred to company (excluding cash)

Estimated yield as a % (say base rate + 1.25%)

0

Calculation of super profits

Estimated projected maintainable profits

-

Less: Yield on capital investment

-

Less: Deemed manager's salary

Super profit

-

Goodwill calculation

Enter profit multiplier (typcally between 2.5 and 3.5)

-

Less: Personal element (say 20%)

Goodwill valuation

-

Note:

We believe the following factors create a conservative valuation:

1. Maintainable profits

2. Manager's salary

3. Multiplier

4. Personal goodwill

Price adjuster clause

The value attributed to the goodwilll may be amended after completion by agreement between the buyer and the seller if a different value is later determined to be the market value of the goodwill at completion. The agreed amendment shall be that which is required to ensure that the value attributed to the goodwill is the market value of the goodwill at completion. Such agreed amendment to the value of the goodwill shall be treated as a variation of the purchase price and the amount outstanding in the loan account shall therefore be reduced or increased as appropriate to take into account the amount of the agreed amendment to the purchase price.

CGT EIS deferral relief claim

Investing in enterprise investment scheme (EIS) shares gives you an opportunity to defer capital gains tax (CGT) that would otherwise be payable.

HOW TO QUALIFY

EIS deferral relief, sometimes referred to as EIS reinvestment relief, can be used to delay and ultimately (sometimes) reduce a CGT bill which has arisen from the sale or transfer of any type of asset. If you sell an asset and reinvest the proceeds in qualifying EIS shares, you can claim EIS deferral relief.

To qualify for deferral relief, your EIS investment must be made between one year before and three years after selling or disposing of the assets which produced the gain. There's no maximum or minimum amount of investment required to qualify for EIS deferral relief (in contrast to EIS income tax relief).

When you sell some or all of the EIS investment, a corresponding proportion of the deferred gain becomes chargeable again.

Example. In November 2014 Harry sold his holiday home on which he made a capital gain of £50,000. He declares this gain on his 2014/15 tax return and is due to pay the resulting CGT on 31 January 2016. But in December 2014 he invests £39,000 in an EIS. This means he can defer tax on £39,000 of the gain. And because the remaining £11,000 is covered by his CGT annual exemption, Harry will have no tax to pay.

In May 2016 Harry sells half his EIS investment. This means that half the deferred gain from the sale of his holiday home, i.e. £19,500, becomes chargeable to CGT for 2016/17.

CGT EIS DEFERRAL RELIEF CLAIM

HM Revenue & Customs

…………………………………… *(insert tax office address)*
……………………………………
……………………………………
……………………………………

…………………………………… *(insert date)*

Dear Sir

…………………………………… **(insert your tax reference)**

Claim For Capital Gains EIS Deferral Relief

Re: Disposal of ………………………… *(insert details of the disposal)* dated ………………… *(insert date of disposal)*

In accordance with Sch 5B of the Taxation of Chargeable Gains Act 1992, I wish to defer the capital gain of ………………… *(insert amount of gain)* on my disposal of the above mentioned assets as I have invested the proceeds into:

…………………………………… *(insert number and details of EIS shares acquired)* on
…………………………………… *(insert date of purchase of EIS shares).*

We attach a computation of the capital gain to be deferred and the completed *EIS3* or EIS5** certificate.

Yours faithfully

………………………

(* The company in which the investment is made must supply you with the EIS3 certificate showing the amount of your investment elgible for CGT deferral relief. If you invested through a fund or investment manager they will issue an EIS5 instead.)

Claim for loss on irrecoverable

loan to a trader

If you've made a loan to a business and it has subsequently been written off or cannot be repaid, then it may be treated as a capital loss which you can use to reduce your captial gains tax (CGT) bill. This doesn't happen automatically, so you will need to submit a claim.

WHAT LOANS QUALIFY?

The loan will qualify for loss relief as long as it was used by the UK resident borrower (who can't be your spouse) in their trade (excluding money lending). A qualifying loan can include a director's loan to a close company.

WHAT DOES IRRECOVERABLE MEAN?

You'll need to show that there was no reasonable prospect of the loan ever being repaid. HMRC's view is that if the borrower continrues to trade, then there is still a chance they could repay the loan; however, this can be challenged if you can show that there was no reasonable prospect of the loan being repaid.

TIME LIMIT?

There's no time limit in which to make a claim. The loss relief will be due at the time you make the claim or, if you prefer, up to two years previously. For example, if you make a claim in 2014/15, you may ask to claim relief in 2012/13 or 2013/14 providing the loan was irrecoverable at that time.

HMRC Helpsheet 296 (http://www.hmrc.gov.uk/helpsheets/hs296.pdf) provides more guidance on making a claim.

CLAIM FOR LOSS ON IRRECOVERABLE LOAN TO A TRADER

HMRC

.... *(insert address)*

....

....

....

.... *(insert date)*

Dear Sirs

.... ***(insert your name)***

.... ***(insert your ten digit tax reference)***

I hereby claim capital loss relief under the provisions of s.253(3) of the Taxation of Chargeable Gains Act 1992 in respect of a loan of £ .... *(insert loan amount)*, made to .... *(insert name and address of trader/trading company)* for use in his trade on the grounds that the loan has now become irrecoverable.

I would like the loss to be treated as arising in the ....*(insert current or previous two tax years)*.

Yours faithfully

.... *(insert signature)*

Election to transfer gain or loss to other group company

Where a company makes a capital gain or loss in respect of an asset, it may jointly elect with another company within the same group to transfer the gain or loss to that company. The effect of an election can be to reduce the overall corporation tax payable by the group.

WHEN TO USE THIS ELECTION

The election can apply to deemed gains or losses, i.e. no transfer or sale of an asset is required. For example, it can apply where a loss is deemed to arise because an asset has become of negligible value. Plus, since 2011 it can also apply to gains or losses resulting from a company leaving a group (a degrouping charge).

HOW TO MAKE AN ELECTION

- the transferor and transferee companies must make an election in writing jointly
- a director or company secretary for each company must sign the election. This can be the same person if they are an officer of both companies
- it must be made within two years of the end of the accounting period of the transferring company
- companies can choose to transfer all of a gain or loss, or part of it.

While an election can stand alone, each company's self-assessment corporation tax returns should include details of the transfer and the effect it has on their respective tax bills.

WITHDRAWAL OF AN ELECTION

An election can be withdrawn within the same time limit that applies for making an election.

ELECTION TO TRANSFER GAIN OR LOSS TO OTHER GROUP COMPANY

HMRC

....*(insert address)*

....

....

....

....*(insert date)*

Dear Sirs

....*(insert name of first company and tax reference)* **(the Transferor)**

....*(insert name of second company and tax reference)* **(the Transferee)**

On ...... *(insert date of disposal)* a chargeable gain/allowable loss* of £........ accrued to the Transferor in respect of assets detailed in the Appendix to this letter.

On behalf of the Transferor and the Transferee, who are members of the same group, we hereby elect under s.171A(4) of the Taxation of Chargeable Gains Act 1992 that the gain/loss[1]* is transferred from the Transferor to the Transferee.

We confirm that s.171(1) of the Taxation of Chargeable Gains Act 1992 would have applied to an actual transfer of the asset from [Transferor] to [Transferee].

Details of the gain/loss* being transferred are shown in the schedule below.

Yours faithfully

....*(insert signature)*

on behalf of *(insert name of first company)*

....*(insert signature)*

on behalf of *(insert name of second company)*

Schedule of gains and losses to be transferred

Name of company	Accounting period	Amount of gain/loss

Appendix: Details of assets disposed of

Asset description

[1]The election may specify a transfer of part of the gain or loss.
* Delete as appropriate.

Gift relief pro forma

When you transfer business assets, e.g. shares in your trading company, to someone other than your spouse at undervalue, you can claim gift relief to defer part or all of the CGT liability. The amount of the gift relief will depend on the amount, if any, of consideration you receive for the asset. Use the gift relief pro forma to help you calculate the amount of gift relief you can claim.

GIFT RELIEF

If you are giving away a business asset, you can claim gift (or holdover) relief. This relief defers the capital gains tax (CGT) on the gift by transferring the liability to the recipient. When the recipient eventually sells the gift, the full CGT bill will normally fall due then and the recipient, rather than you, will have to pay it. The claim is made on the form at the end of HMRC Helpsheet HS295 (http://www.hmrc.gov.uk/helpsheets/hs295.pdf).

PARTIAL CONSIDERATION

Where you receive some payment for the transfer of the asset but this is less than market value, then the gift relief claim may need to be restricted. Your taxable gain will be the actual cash profit you make on the gift.

Example. Jenny bought a property for use in her trade in May 2001 for £50,000. In October 2015 Jenny transferred the property to Thomas when it was worth £200,000. Thomas pays Jenny £100,000 for the property. Jenny has made a cash profit of £50,000 (£100,000 - £50,000) so this is the amount of her taxable gain. The amount of gift relief will be the market value less the original cost less the taxable gain, i.e. £100,000 (£200,000 - £50,000 - £50,000).

Note. Where full gift relief is available (i.e. you are not receiving consideration greater than the asset's original cost), the market value figure at the date of gift is irrelevent as none of the gain remains chargeable in the year of the gift. In this case, no formal valuation is necessary at the time of the transfer - there is a box on Helpsheet HS295 to request the valuation to be deferred. However, a valuation will be necessary where the amount of the gift relief is restricted.

TIME LIMIT

The time limit for gift relief is four years from the end of the tax year of disposal. Therefore, for a gift in the 2014/15 tax year, a gift relief claim is only valid if it's made on or before 5 April 2019.

GIFT RELIEF PRO FORMA

Capital gains tax computation for transferor

Deemed proceeds, i.e. market value of asset

Less: costs of transfer, e.g. legal fees

£   -

Less: cost of acquisition (or market value as at
31 March 1982 if the asset was acquired prior to this date)

Less: enhancement expenditure

Deemed capital gain

£   -

Actual proceeds, i.e. amount paid to you by transferee

Capital gain held over

£   -

Capital gain chargeable on transferor

£   -

Deemed cost of asset for transferee

£   -

Plus: costs of acquisition, e.g. legal fees

Less: holdover relief relief

£   -

Revised cost of new asset for CGT purposes

£   -

Negligible value claim

If you own an asset that has become of negligible value, i.e. worthless, you can make a negligible value claim to HMRC which will enable you to write off the asset as a capital loss. You can offset this loss against other gains and thereby reduce your CGT bill.

LOSSES ON SHARES

You may have made an investment in the past that has performed badly. Indeed, you may have written it off in your own mind but, if you haven't sold it, it may only be a paper loss that is not allowable for CGT purposes. However, there is an exception to the normal rule whereby you may be able to establish an allowable capital loss to offset against a capital gain even though there hasn't been an actual disposal. If you can persuade HMRC that the shares are virtually worthless, e.g. the company has ceased trading and is insolvent, you can make a **Negligible Value Claim** to offset this loss against your capital gains to reduce the amount of CGT you pay.

NEGLIGIBLE VALUE LIST

HMRC keeps a list of quoted shares that are recognised as being of negligible value (see http://hmrc.gov.uk/cgt/negvalist.htm).

CHECKING NEGLIGIBLE VALUE

HMRC operates a post-transaction valuation service for capital gains, which is accessed by submitting Form CG34 (http://www.hmrc.gov.uk/forms/cg34.pdf) to HMRC. You can also use this service to check if an asset has become of negligible value. Submit the Form CG34 at the same time as your negligible value claim.

TIME LIMIT

You can make a negligible value claim at any time after the shares have become worthless. Therefore, defer a claim until there are sufficient gains to avoid you wasting your annual exemption. The shares will be treated as though you sold them on the date you made the claim or up to two years before the tax year in which you make the claim (as long as they were worthless at the time).

NEGLIGIBLE VALUE CLAIM

HMRC

.... *(insert address)*

....

....

....

.... *(insert date)*

Dear Sirs

Negligible value claim

.... ***(insert your name)***

.... ***(insert your ten digit tax reference)***

I claim relief under s.24(2) of the Taxation of Chargeable Gains Act 1992 for the tax year ended 5 April ..... *(insert year)* in respect of my shareholding in ......*(insert company name)* Ltd/plc which cost £..... *(insert figure)* on ..... *(insert purchase date)*.

*[The shares are included on the "negligible value list" maintained by the Shares and Assets Valuation Office and were of negligible value as at the date of this claim].

*[The shares are not currently included on the "negligible value list" but I believe the shares are of negligible value and, therefore, enclose form CG34 for the Shares and Assets Valuation team to agree this].

Please could you acknowledge receipt of this claim.

Yours faithfully

……………………………………. *(insert signature)*

* delete as appropriate

Rollover relief claim

When you've sold an asset that was used in your business, and this results in a capital gain, it's possible to avoid tax on this by claiming rollover relief.

SELLING A BUSINESS ASSET

Capital gains tax (CGT) applies to profit you make when you sell a business asset. If this results in a CGT bill you have the option to make a **Rollover Relief Claim** to roll over the gain into the purchase of another business asset and so defer payment of tax.

QUALIFYING ASSETS

Rollover relief is only available on the sale of qualifying business assets. This includes business goodwill, land and buildings and fixed plant and machinery. Unfortunately, shares are not a qualifying asset.

AMOUNT OF RELIEF

Where relief is claimed it's said to be rolled over because it's deducted from the cost of the replacement asset, therefore increasing the gain or reducing the loss when it's sold. The amount of rollover relief depends on whether you fully invest the proceeds of the sale. If you only re-invest part of the proceeds, then the relief will be restricted to the amount re-invested.

TIME LIMITS

The replacement asset must be acquired within a period starting one year before and three years after the date of the disposal of the original asset. The time limit for making the rollover relief claim is four years from the end of the tax year in which the old asset was sold.

ROLLOVER RELIEF CLAIM

HMRC

....*(insert address)*

....

....

....

....*(insert date)*

Dear Sirs

.... *(insert your name)*

....*(insert your ten digit tax reference)*

.....................*(insert business name or asset description)* was sold for £ ……….. *(insert sale proceeds)* on ……..*(insert date).* Proceeds of £ ……. *(insert amount re-invested)* were reinvested in the purchase of ...………………………………………......*(insert new business name or asset description)* on ………….. *(insert date).* Both the asset sold and the asset acquired fall into the class of assets set out in s.155 of the Taxation of Chargeable Gains Act 1992.

Please accept this letter as a formal claim under s.152 of the Taxation of Chargeable Gains Act 1992 that the chargeable gain arising on the disposal is rolled over and that the base cost is reduced accordingly.

Yours faithfully

....*(insert signature)*

Rollover relief pro forma

When you've sold an asset that was used in your business, and this results in a capital gain, it's possible to avoid tax on this by claiming rollover relief.

SELLING A BUSINESS ASSET

Capital gains tax (CGT) applies to profit you make when you sell a business asset. If this results in a CGT bill you have the option to make a claim to roll over the gain into the purchase of another business asset and so defer payment of tax.

QUALIFYING ASSETS

Rollover relief is only available on the sale of qualifying business assets. This includes business goodwill, land and buildings and fixed plant and machinery. Unfortunately, shares are not a qualifying asset.

AMOUNT OF RELIEF

Where relief is claimed it's said to be rolled over because it's deducted from the cost of the replacement asset, therefore increasing the gain or reducing the loss when it's sold. The amount of rollover relief depends on whether you fully invest the proceeds of the sale. If you only re-invest part of the proceeds, then the relief will be restricted to the amount re-invested. Use the **Rollover Relief Pro Forma** to calculate the base cost of the replacement asset.

ROLLOVER RELIEF PRO FORMA

Capital gains tax computation on sale of business assets

Sales proceeds

Less: costs of sale

£   -

Less: cost of acquisition (or market value as at
31 March 1982 if the asset was acquired prior to this date)

Less: enhancement expenditure

Capital gain   £   -

Adjustment percentage to acount for non-business use of asset

Amount of proceeds that can qualify for rollover relief   £   -

Amount of proceeds used to buy new buisness assets

Rollover relief   £   -

Chargeable gain after rollover relief   £   -

Cost of new asset   £   -

Plus: costs of acquisition

Less: rollover relief   -

Revised cost of new asset for CGT purposes   £   -

Share valuation pro forma

When you gift, or transfer at undervalue, shares in your trading company to anyone other than your spouse, it is deemed to have been made at fair market value and will be liable to CGT (although you may be able to claim gift relief to defer the gain). Therefore, you will often need to value the shares at the time of the transfer. Use the share valuation pro forma as a useful guide to help you do this.

VALUING SHARES - EARNINGS BASIS

The most common method adopted for valuing shares in trading companies is to use a multiple of maintainable or "super" profits. Maintainable profits are those below which the future profits are unlikely to fall, in the absence of exceptional circumstances.

ADJUSTMENTS TO PROFITS

It may be necessary to make adjustments to the profits to reflect commercial charges, for items such as directors' remuneration. Adjustments to profits are usually made to substitute commercial charges for any non-commercial ones and to remove the effects of exceptional or extraordinary items.

WEIGHTED AVERAGE

The earnings figure will often be calculated by reference to an average, or weighted average, of a number of years' past profits, usually three or four years. However, if the past profit levels bear no relation to the maintainable profits, then the average of past profits may not be an appropriate basis.

WHICH MULTIPLE?

Very often valuations for tax purposes are of minority holdings. A common method used for this purpose is the application of a price earnings or P/E ratio, from a comparable quoted company (or sector average), to the earnings per share of the unquoted company, from which a discount of up to about 80% for a small uninfluential minority holding may be applied.

SHARE VALUATION PRO FORMA

Company name

Valuation date

Percentage shareholding:

Step 1 - Calculating "super" profits

Accounting year and results

Enter year of most recent accounts

	£	£	£	£

Profit per accounts
(prior to dividends but after corporation tax)

Add back:

Directors' remuneration

Employers' paid NI on remuneration
Other items that have distorted profit:
e.g. one-off loss

Adjusted profit   -   -   -   -

Less:

Manager's salary (include a manager's
salary for each working director)

Employers' NI on manager's salary   -   -   -   -

Other items that have distorted profit:

e.g. capital gain

"Super" profits (unweighted)   -   -   -   -

Weighting multiple*
(weight is given to most recent results)

Weighted average super profits   -   -   -   -

Step 2 - Calculating the value of the company

Weighted average super profit	Estimated Profit to earnings ratio	Value of company
(A)	(B)	(AxB)
£		£
0		-

Step 3 - Valuation of actual shareholding

	£	£
Your shareholding	0%	-
Less:		
Discount for minority shareholding:		-
Valuation		-

* A typical weighting ratio would be 4 for the most recent accounts then 3,2 and 1

Trading loss relief claim

If you've made a loss in your sole trade or partnership and you're unable to make full use of that loss against your total income, the balance can be set against your capital gains in the year of the loss or the previous year. Relief is not given automatically, so you'll need to make a trading loss relief claim.

TRADING LOSSES

You can't offset capital losses against your general income in a tax year. However, you can reduce your capital gains by offsetting sole trader or partnership trading losses which you haven't been able to offset against other income.

MAKING A CLAIM

This **Trading Loss Relief Claim** should not be made on its own - it should be made at the same time as a claim to offset the current year's trading loss against other total income for the year of loss and/or the previous tax year (**s.64 ITA 2007** claim). An s.64 claim against income of the year must be made first, in full, up to the amount of other income (unfortunately, in many instances this can result in the personal allowance being wasted).

HOW MUCH OF THE LOSS CAN BE OFFSET?

The amount of the trading loss which can be set against the capital gain is the lower of the "relevant amount" and the "maximum amount". The "relevant amount" is the amount of trading loss that is left over after the s.64 claim has been dealt with (possibly because there is not enough income to fully utilise the loss); the "maximum amount" is the amount of capital gains arising in the year less the capital losses of the same year and unrelieved capital losses brought forward. Once that lower amount has been calculated, it is allowed in the computation before other capital losses brought forward or carried back and definitely before the annual exemption (which may, again, be wasted).

TIME LIMIT

The claim must be made within twelve months of 31 January following the end of the tax year in which the loss arose. For example, 31 January 2017 for a loss incurred in the 2014/15 tax year.

TRADING LOSS RELIEF CLAIM

HMRC

....*(insert address)*

....

....

....

....*(insert date)*

Dear Sirs

....***(insert your name)***

....***(insert your ten digit tax reference)***

In the tax year ended 5 April ..... *(insert year)*, my business made a loss of £ ....*(insert amount)*. In accordance with the provisions of s.64(2) ITA 2007, I elect for £ ....*(insert amount)* of this loss to be offset against my other income in the tax year ended 5 April ..... *(insert year)*.

In the tax year ended 5 April ...... *(insert year)*, I also made capital gains (after deducting allowable losses) of £ ..... *(insert amount)*. In accordance with the provisions of s.71, ITA 2007, I elect for £ ..... *(insert amount)* of the trading loss to be offset against these gains.

Please could you acknowledge receipt of this claim.

Yours faithfully

....*(insert signature)*

Section 3

Dealing with tax investigations

Amending a tax return

If HMRC considers that there's something wrong with your tax return, but doesn't think it's deliberate, it will normally write asking you to amend it within 30 days of its notification. If you agree with the change, what's the most foolproof way of dealing with it?

ALLOWED TO AMEND

At the end of an enquiry, if HMRC finds nothing wrong with your return, it should advise you of this and write to say so in a closure notice. However, if it considers that there's something wrong with your tax return, but doesn't think you have done this deliberately, it will normally write asking you to make an amendment; this has to be done within 30 days of the notification. Use our **Amending a Tax Return** letter for a foolproof way to do this, which will lead to a revision of your tax liability for the year concerned, with an interest charge on any resulting underpayment or interest payable to you on any overpayment.

AMENDING A TAX RETURN

HMRC

.... *(insert your tax office)*

.... *(insert address)*

.... *(insert your name)*

.... *(insert your address)*

.... *(insert date)*

Dear Sirs

Subject: Amendment to Personal Tax Return   *(insert tax year)*

Name: *(insert your name)*

UTR: *(insert the ten digit unique tax reference on the return)*

NI number: *(insert your NI number)*

As I filed my return on time, I am entitled to amend that return within twelve months of the filing date under s9ZA **Taxes Management Act 1970**.

This letter is to formally advise you that I have identified an entry or entries on that return that require revision. I would be grateful if you would deal with the following revision(s) as soon as possible.

Kindly change the entries on my file for:

1. .... *(insert further information concerning an entry on your return).*

2. *(Entry "X" amended to entry "Y". Your stipulated amendment can be in the form of a narrative describing a change to contents of a particular box on that return or enclosing an amended return or an extra supplementary page or an amended supplementary page).*

(Remember that if your change affects your tax (or Class 4 NI) liability you should also amend the tax (or Class 4 NI) due.

I would be grateful if you could acknowledge receipt of this letter and its contents.

Please could you issue me with a revised tax calculation.

Yours faithfully

.... *(insert signature)*

Appeal and postponement of direct tax

This standard letter can be used to make an appeal against any direct tax assessment, e.g. income tax, corporation tax, capital gains tax etc., but not VAT, customs or other duties.

HOW TO USE IT

The time limit for submitting an appeal is 30 days from the date on the assessment or determination issued by HMRC. The letter should be sent direct to the issuing tax office or, if different, to the office that you usually communicate with in relation to the type of tax assessed.

The postponement section of the letter is optional. Only use this part if you don't intend to pay the full amount of the disputed tax. It's advisable to include a calculation showing how you arrived at the figure of tax you consider is payable, if any. You may choose to pay the assessment in full to avoid interest charges on the disputed tax in the event that you lose the appeal.

APPEAL AND POSTPONEMENT OF DIRECT TAX

HM Revenue and Customs

....*(insert address)*
....
....
....

....*(insert date)*

....*(insert HMRC reference)*

Dear Sir

Notice of appeal and application to postpone tax

....***(insert your name and tax reference or National Insurance number)***

Please accept this letter as a notice of appeal against the following tax assessment/determination:

Assessment reference number: ....

Year or period covered by assessment: ....

Type of charge (e.g. income tax, corporation tax, penalty charge) ....

Amount of tax, duty etc. charged   £................................

Reason for the appeal

I/we believe that the assessment/determination *(delete as appropriate)* is incorrect because:

....
....

....
....
....

(Continue on separate sheet if there's insufficient room to explain your reasons for the appeal.)

Postponement of tax application

I/we believe that the tax shown as payable by the assessment/determination is excessive and should be reduced as follows pending settlement of my/our appeal *(delete as applicable)*.

Tax/penalty etc. due according to assessment   £ ....

Tax that I/we wish to postpone   £ ....

Tax remaining payable   £ ....

My/our calculation of tax remaining payable is attached *(don't forget to attach your calculations to this letter).*

I/we look forward to receiving your acknowledgment of this appeal [and application to postpone payment of the tax/penalty charged].

Yours faithfully

....*(insert signature)*

....*(insert name)*

Capital statement checklist

In larger investigation cases, HMRC may require a so-called capital statement to be prepared. Use our checklist to present this to your best advantage.

WHAT IS A CAPITAL STATEMENT?

If there is difficulty in obtaining business records for earlier years, any attempt to recalculate omissions fairly precisely for individual periods will usually rely on the capital/income/expenditure reconciliation method, i.e. capital statements. A capital statement is prepared on the basis that an individual's personal expenditure added to any increase/decrease in wealth during the period must equal total income during that period.

If personal expenditure taken with the movement in assets results in a total which is more than total declared income, HMRC will assume that the deficiency is undeclared business profits unless there is another satisfactory explanation. For more information on HMRC's approach to capital statements, see section EM3580 of its enquiry manual (http://www.hmrc.gov.uk/manuals/emmanual/EM3580.htm).

Every capital statement will be different but our **Capital Statement Checklist** is intended to be a guide to the types of item which must be considered.

CAPITAL STATEMENT CHECKLIST

Capital statement for ....(*insert name*)

Assets and liabilities as at .... (*insert date*)

Private income and expenditure for the period/year ended.....................(*insert year*)

Non-business assets

Asset	Notes	Asset value (£)
Property	Private residence (watch for any changes in and ensure that expenses are picked up and any profit/loss properly dealt with)	
	Holiday home, let property, time share	
Investments		
Bank accounts	Non-business current and deposit accounts, in names of husband, wife and children	
Building society accounts - as above		
Unquoted shares		
Quoted shares		
Settlements made	(see note 4)	
Unit trust holdings		
Investment bonds		
Premium bonds		
National savings bonds and certificates		
Cash	The existence of any substantial hoards	
Loan accounts	Balances on all company loan accounts	
Loans to/from friends, family and associates		

Asset	Notes	Asset value (£)
Other assets:		
Used in the business	But not reflected on the balance sheet	
Antiques and paintings	Valuable items only	
	Normal household furnishings and antiques should be shown in expenditure in relevant year	
Cars	Vehicles held outside the business	
Boats		
Private plane/helicopter		
Birds/fish/other animals	Valuable items only	
Horses	Racing and show jumping	
Total value of non business assets		

Note 1. In all cases keep a note of the actual cost price of the asset including incidental costs of acquisition. A copy of the invoice would help.

Note 2. Where an asset is sold during the year any profit on sale is taken to income. Any loss and incidental sale expenses are taken to expenses.

Note 3. Where unusual assets are held, make a note to pick up all running expenses and incidental income.

Note 4. Gifts should be included only where the individual retains an interest. Other settlements can be shown as expenditure in the relevant year.

Non-business liabilities

Liability	Notes	Value of liability (£)
Mortgages		
Bank loans		
Credit card balances		
Company loan accounts		
Hire purchase debts		
Loans from associates, family and friends		
Total value of non-business liabilities		

Private income

Source of income	Notes	Amount (£)
Drawings from a business		
Salary	(See note 1)	
Bonuses and commissions from employment		
Spouse's earnings	(See note 1)	
Redundancy/severance		
Income from investments		
Rents received		
Interest received		
Dividends		
Proceeds from sale of assets		
Premium bond winnings		

Source of income	Notes	Amount (£)
Lottery winnings		
Cash gifts	Wherever possible large gifts should be substantiated by independent evidence	
Proceeds of life assurance policies		
Insurance recoveries		
Gambling wins		
Prize money		
Income tax repayments		
Social security benefits		
Total private income		

Note 1. If the payments are regular, under deduction of tax show the net sum received. Otherwise show the gross amount and ensure PAYE is shown as an expense (see private expenditure checklist). Watch consistency of treatment with director's loan account.

Private expenditure

Description	Notes	Amount (£)
For detail see separate private expenditure checklist		
Total private expenditure		

Capital statement

	£
Balance (assets less liabilities) at start of period	
Add: Private income	
Add: Net business income (declared on tax return)	
Deduct: Private expenditure	
Add net unrealised increase/decrease in market value of investments	
Balance (assets less liabilities) at end of period	

Changing interview notes

If you attend an enquiry interview, the tax inspector will make their own notes of what they "think" was said and use them against you if they can. They will probably try to get you to sign them as a true record of what came up at the meeting. Should you?

READ THE NOTES

Never sign notes at a meeting. Gain yourself some thinking time by saying you would like to go over the notes in some detail. Ask the inspector to send them to you. Go through the notes looking for all the things that are wrong, both where they do not reflect what was said and where they do but you have since discovered that what was said was incorrect. The latter is one way of changing your mind after the event, particularly if an off-the-cuff remark is not confirmed by what you find in your records. Even when you send the amended notes back to HMRC, don't sign but do include our **Changing Interview Notes** covering letter.

CHANGING INTERVIEW NOTES

………………………………..…(*insert name*)

HMRC

……………………………….. (*insert address*)

……………………………………

……………………………….. (*insert date*)

Dear ……………………………….. (*insert name*)

……………………………….. (***insert name and tax reference***)

Thank you for your letter dated ….. (*insert date*) containing your notes from our meeting held on ….. (*insert date*).

I/we have been through the notes looking for instances where they do not reflect what we recollect as being said and/or where they do but I/we have since discovered that what was said was incorrect (for example an off the cuff remark has not been confirmed by what I/we you found in our records).

In particular (e.g. the adjustments agreed to at the interview which appear to be too high are ….)

I/we have annotated the enclosed copy of the notes accordingly.

However, we are unable to sign the interview notes in accordance with the best practice established following the Wall v IRC case. I/we trust you will not object to this.

Yours sincerely

. (*insert signature*)

Checklist for attacking a business economics exercise

In the pursuit of tax collection targets there is now a much greater willingness by HMRC to displace the profits shown by your accounts with an estimate based on a simple business economics exercise. Our checklist can help you identify flaws in the tax inspector's calculations.

MISSING INCOME?

A typical example of a business economics exercise would be for HMRC to use a mark-up of purchases to selling price and construct an anticipated sales figure. The next stage is to compare that with the sales shown in the accounts. The difference is, in his view, missing income! The scope for inaccuracies in such an exercise is vast so HMRC's calculations need to be attacked, not only in terms of the detailed figures employed, but also of the overall credibility of the ratios used, e.g. gross profit percentage.

ATTACKING HMRC'S ARGUMENT

Firstly, you have to get hold of the tax inspector's calculations. Write and say that you recognise they have done a lot of work and research to arrive at their reconstruction results. However, could they kindly provide details of their calculations? From here you can start to pick holes in their argument line by line, not accepting any assumption. Use our **Checklist for Attacking a Business Economics Exercise** (or reconstruction as it is sometimes known) to help you do this.

CHECKLIST FOR ATTACKING A
BUSINESS ECONOMICS EXERCISE

The tax inspector's calculations	Actioned
Write to the tax inspector and say that you recognise he has done a lot of work and research to arrive at his reconstruction results. However, could he kindly provide details of his calculations. Once received, check all the calculations the tax inspector provides, line by line. Are they mathematically correct?	
Representative period? Is the period chosen by the tax inspector in his calculations truly representative of the business' trading year? Check that it excludes, say, exceptionally busy or quiet periods.	
Product mix Does the business sell more than one item? If yes, then establish the product mix, i.e. the range of products sold and in what proportion. Do this for a sample period, e.g. three months from a review of purchase invoices. **Note.** Changes in product mix over the year can also be taken into account to undermine his calculation.	
Purchase invoices Make sure only purchases for resale are included and check whether items such as goods for own use and ancillary items such as packaging have been excluded.	
Prices Where did the tax inspector get his prices? In a trading account reconstruction much hinges on using the price at the time, not current prices. With the help of an actual price list can you cast doubt on the prices the inspector has used. **Note.** You might not remember what the prices were but you can often find some supporting evidence. For example, copies of old pricing policies, price lists, analysis codes on till rolls, recommended retail prices as shown on the invoices. If you have an old price list, the inspector will not be justified in substituting his own figures.	
Is his calculation too rigid? Life is not that simple, there are many factors that can impinge on these calculations, e.g. theft and wastage to mention only two. You can expect both of these in the real world.	

The tax inspector's calculations	Actioned
Are the tax inspector's figures the maximum achievable? Has he given credit for wastage/losses?	
Gross profit percentage Where the main activity of the business consists of the purchase and resale of goods, the tax inspector will concentrate on the relationship between these two figures. The formulae most often used are: Gross profit rate (GPR) = (gross profit/sales) x 100 and mark-up rate (MUR) = (GPR/(100 – GPR)) x 100. For example, the GPR will be compared with the GPR of the same business in previous years and the GPR of similar businesses in the area.	
Other business ratios Where the business does not consist of the purchase of goods for resale, the inspector will look for some other direct relationship between expenses and turnover to give him some indication of the reliability of the return. Examples of such ratios are fuel to takings, e.g. in the case of a taxi driver or driving instructor or food to takings, e.g. in the case of a restaurant or hotel. If there is no relationship, the factors considered may include overall profitability, time spent by the proprietor and turnover expressed as an hourly/daily rate. In these circumstances put forward your own ratio that you believe best represents the business and your reasons for selecting it.	

Complaint letter

Ultimately, the Adjudicator's Office handles all complaints about HMRC. However, the adjudicator will only examine a complaint if it has been through the proper levels of authority within HMRC first. It's the same letter but to different people. So what should you put in this particular piece of correspondence?

SET OUT YOUR GRIEVANCE

If you feel you have been unfairly treated by HMRC, for example unreasonable delays, mistakes or poorly treated by staff, the avenues of complaint are to: **(1)** an HMRC complaints handler; **(2)** review by a different complaints handler; **(3)** the Adjudicator; and **(4)** the Parliamentary and Health Service Ombudsman. Your complaint should set out exactly what is being sought - an apology, an explanation with an assurance that it will not happen again and an itemised request for compensation. You can use our **Complaint Letter** to set out your grievance to the relevant person.

Note. If you don't agree with an HMRC decision, such as the amount of tax you've been asked to pay, then you'll need to follow the review and appeals process instead.

COMPLAINT LETTER

[The Complaints Handler]

....*(insert address of Tax Office you have been dealing with)*

....

....

....

....*(insert date)*

Dear Sir

Formal complaint

....***(insert name and tax reference)***

It is with regret that I/we must write to you complaining of the way in which ..... *(insert name of Inspector or other revenue official involved)* has acted in the handling of my/our tax affairs.

[I am/we are sure that if you were able to listen to recordings of telephone conversations between me/us and the officer concerned, including the one in which I/we allege he [swore/was intimidating/gave misleading advice/refused to take my complaint seriously/was talking at cross purposes] you would uphold my/our complaint without question. That conversation has caused me considerable worry and distress since.]

It says in [your Code of Practice ..... *(insert reference)*, HMRC manual ....*(insert reference)*, Statement of Practice ..... *(insert reference)*,] that you will .... *(insert action)*. However, in this case you have not done so.

Overall, I/we consider that there have been unreasonable delays in dealing with correspondence. In particular it took .... *(insert number of weeks)* to provide me with an answer about .... *(insert question)*.

There were other delays in [replying to correspondence/finalising tax adjustments/notifying me of the results of the internal technical review/replying to my request for a closure notification]. These delays added to my worry and distress over the investigation.

With this letter I am/we are seeking [an apology/an explanation/an assurance it will not happen again] and enclose an itemised request for compensation. [Included is a copy of the fee note charged to and settled by me/us from our advisor(s), reimbursement of which would be a tangible recognition (i.e. redress) for the mistakes made by yourselves].

[I have suffered direct financial loss as a result of your mistakes including £..... *(insert figure)* for postage (receipts included), £... *(insert figure)* for telephone calls and £..... *(insert figure)* for delayed resolution of this complaint]. [Out-of-pocket expenses were £..... *(insert figure)*.]

Your Complaints Factsheet (C/FS) clearly states that you will pay compensation, or reimburse costs that arise as a direct result of your mistakes. An interim payment whilst you calculate the total sum to reimburse would be acceptable.

Kindly acknowledge receipt of this letter and its contents as soon as possible.

Yours faithfully

....*(insert signature)*

Enc

Date not convenient letter

HMRC carries out thousands of on-site PAYE inspections every year. The date proposed might not be convenient for you or your payroll staff, yet you don't want to appear evasive, like you have something to hide.

LETTER

Our **Date Not Convenient Letter**, which asks HMRC to rearrange its visit, takes the stress out of having to consider what to say. It strikes the right tone without appearing stuffy or evasive.

DATE NOT CONVENIENT LETTER

HMRC

……………………………… *(insert address)*

……………………………

……………………………

……………………………

……………………………. *(insert date)*

Reference:………………………… *(insert your company's/business's tax reference)*

Dear Sir

…………………………………………. *(insert name of business)*

Thank you for your letter of ………………………….*(insert date)*.

We understand that you wish to carry out an inspection of our PAYE records on………………… *(insert date)*. Unfortunately due to [staff holidays, the absence of a key member of staff, staff commitments for stock taking/financial year end procedures etc.] it will not be convenient for you to start the inspection on the date [any of the dates] suggested.

We would like to assist you in expediting the inspection, and in view of this we suggest that any of the following dates would be suitable………………… *(insert dates)*. Please let us know as soon as possible which, if any, of these will be acceptable for you. We suggest that to settle on a mutually convenient date as soon as possible you should telephone……………… *(insert name of director/partner/member of staff)* to make arrangements.

Yours faithfully

……………………………. *(insert signature)*

Key events chart

If you are subject to a personal tax enquiry, deposits on your bank account statements could be taken to be a second source of income by HMRC. Therefore, it's a good idea to keep an up-to-date record of these rather than relying on your memory, or an expensive exercise by your advisor later.

UNIDENTIFIED BANKINGS

The most common verbal explanations for unidentified bankings, or deficiencies in income when compared with personal expenditure, are: cash savings, gambling winnings, legacies, loans and gifts.

HMRC will probe any such verbal explanation. Its internal manual gives guidance to inspectors on how to deal with claims relating to this type of income and advises that such claims "may sometimes be true" - which indicates the fairly sceptical approach you can expect.

Indeed, if you need to proceed to a tax tribunal, the burden of proof to substantiate such claims will rest with you, not HMRC.

LOG UNUSUAL INCOME

So each tax year you should review private bank statements to make sure that you have valid explanations for all credit entries. It's probably a good idea to do this anyway when preparing/signing off your personal tax return. Ideally, log unusual sources of income on a **Key Events Chart** either at the time they occur or when you are completing your annual tax return. You then have a ready explanation for HMRC should it open an enquiry, without having to launch into a costly investigation exercise.

KEY EVENTS CHART

Date	Amount £	Business	Personal	Documentation
2005	10,000		Loan from parents	Parent's bank statement
2009	50,000	Premises acquired		Bank loan
2011	3,500		Encashed policy	Letter from insurance company
2014	25,000		Inheritance	Letter from solicitor

Letter to get a tax penalty reduced

HMRC has the power to reduce a maximum tax penalty to take account of the nature and quality of any disclosure you have made about an "inaccuracy". How do you get this on the inspector's negotiating agenda?

WHAT WILL TRIGGER A PENALTY?

A tax penalty can now be triggered in two possible ways. Firstly, a document (basically any type of HMRC return) is delivered to HMRC and contains an inaccuracy that leads either to a loss of tax, or to an inflated claim for relief. Secondly, you accept an assessment by HMRC knowing that it's insufficient and take no action (within 30 days) to advise it of your error. No penalty will be charged if it can be shown that the error was due to a simple mistake that did not amount to carelessness. The maximum level of penalty for each offence is a percentage of tax that has been lost to HMRC as a result of the offence.

TAKING ACCOUNT OF DISCLOSURE

Penalties can be reduced by HMRC to take account of the nature and quality of any disclosure made. This does not just mean bringing the matter to its attention "unprompted" but, for example, includes co-operation given in quantifying the error and providing access to records.

"Unprompted disclosure" occurs when you bring the error to HMRC's notice without it being aware of it or having already started an inquiry. Any other type of disclosure will be regarded as prompted but both can make a significant difference to reducing the level of penalty.

HMRC is not allowed, however, to go below a minimum level which the law stipulates. These are as follows:

NATURE OF OFFENCE	MAX	MIN UNPROMPTED	MIN PROMPTED
Genuine mistake despite taking reasonable care	0%	0%	0%
Careless action	30%	0%	15%
Deliberate no concealment	70%	20%	35%
Deliberate with concealment	100%	35%	50%

From this table you can see that there is a significant effect in making a full unprompted disclosure. Even in prompted disclosure situations the level of co-operation will make a large difference to the ultimate penalty level. Use our **Letter to Get a Tax Penalty Reduced** to help you achieve these savings.

LETTER TO GET A TAX PENALTY REDUCED

HMRC

……………………………………….. *(insert address)*
……………………………………….
……………………………………….
……………………………………….
……………………………………….

………………………………………. *(insert date)*

Your reference: ……………………………………

Dear Sir or Madam

Reduction in tax penalty

Further to your letter dated……… *(insert date)* concerning tax geared penalties, we would be grateful you would kindly consider reducing the level of penalty you suggest to take account of the nature and quality of any disclosure already made to you by us. This includes the unprompted disclosure made to you on ……………………….. *(insert date)* (copy enclosed) which brought the matter to your attention, and/or disclosures made to you after the start of your enquiry (copy also enclosed).

We would also like you to take into account the co-operation which was given to you by us in actually quantifying the error in some detail.

We believe that:
- our original disclosure was full and complete and covered not only what the error was but how and why it arose
- we provided full co-operation, enabling the investigation to be concluded as quickly as possible; and
- we allowed HMRC access to records and documents without the need to resort to formal orders.

Guidance in your manual suggests that the reduction that can be made to a penalty will be greatest where you are able to take the above points into account.

We therefore, look forward to hearing from you about a suitable reduction in our penalty.

[(Add if appropriate:)

Request for suspension of penalty

We understand that you have an important power to suspend some or all of any penalty which relates to careless action. We humbly request that you allow this to happen in our particular case and look forward to being informed of the period of this suspension together with the measurable conditions which must be complied with, in order to improve our compliance procedures going forward. We are confident that at the end of the period the conditions will have been satisfied and that you will be in a position to drop the penalty.]

Yours faithfully

………………………………………… (insert name)

………………………………………… *(insert position)*

Encs

No interview letter

There is no statutory obligation to attend an interview with HMRC and some advisors advocate non-attendance. However, how can you persuade your particular tax inspector that this isn't a good idea at this time?

PROBING QUESTIONS

Once they have been through your records, the tax inspector dealing with your enquiry likes to sit down with you and go through a pre-prepared list of questions. They will have already anticipated your answers to some of these and will have more probing follow-up questions to match. The risk at interview is that you might give too much away or just give the wrong answer, all in an attempt to be helpful and get rid of the problem. Therefore, if you don't want to attend an interview, try sending our **No Interview Letter** to the tax inspector dealing with your enquiry.

NO INTERVIEW LETTER

HMRC

.... *(insert address)*

....

....

.... *(insert date)*

Dear Sirs

....*(insert your business name and tax reference)*

Thank you for your letter dated ..... *(insert date)* requesting an interview.

It seems clear that I/we have made no attempt to conceal any income or to overstate any expenditure.

If your review of my/our records has thrown up any matters that appear to you prima facie to be unsatisfactory, there appears to be no reason why such matters cannot be aired in writing. I/we have every confidence that a fully acceptable explanation will be available. Nor do I/we think that there are any areas that you would wish to discuss at a meeting but that could not equally be discussed in correspondence.

Moreover, this enquiry has already involved me/us in a great deal of unnecessary expense, and attendance at a meeting would not only add to this expense but could also result in a fairly considerable loss of income.

If, therefore, there are any relevant matters on which you would like additional information, I/we should be pleased if you would specify them, and we will continue to do all I/we can towards bringing this enquiry to an end in the shortest possible time.

In the absence of any suggestion of wrongdoing, however, and for the reasons given above, I/we do not feel that our interests would be best served by interrupting my/our working procedures in order to attend a meeting.

It should also be pointed out that it is not always true to say that "meetings are far more cost-effective and far less time-consuming than dealing with matters by correspondence". Questions of detail might well be impossible to answer from memory across the desk, so that I/we would still have to go away, look up the points, and reply in writing.

Yours faithfully

.... *(insert signature)*

Obligation for past event

One tax game that's played every year end involves getting tax relief before you've spent any money. Quite often you don't get the actual invoice in before the year-end. So instead you can include in your accounts a reasonable provision for the estimated costs of what you will eventually pay. However, what evidence would HMRC expect to find about this?

SIGNIFICANT PROVISIONS

A reasonable provision in your accounts for the estimated costs of what you will eventually pay is an accepted accounting principle. And, as such, it is clearly recognised by HMRC as tax deductible. However, in order to include a provision in your accounts, certain conditions need to be met under the Financial Reporting Standards. Put simply, you need *"an obligation at the reporting date as a result of a past event"* **(s.21.4 FRS 102)**. Use our **Obligation for Past Event** file note to fend off any challenge from HMRC as to the legitimacy of significant provisions in your accounts.

OBLIGATION FOR PAST EVENT

File note

In our opinion the Company has an obligation at the balance sheet date as a result of a past event. Therefore in accordance with [Financial Reporting Standard 12 (FRS 12)] or [s.21.4 FRS 102], we have decided to include a provision in the Company's accounts for the year/period ended ......*(insert date)*. We have examined the evidence available to us and are satisfied that this meets the conditions of FRS 12/FRS 102 as follows:

Condition 1. There is an obligation at the balance sheet date as a result of a past event.

The past event was [e.g. wear and tear on the building caused by the Company's use of it] and the current obligation is [e.g. the new legislation /dilapidations clause in a lease etc.]. To be prudent we must presume that the Company will have to incur expenditure, as there is no evidence to suggest that it won't.

Condition 2. It is known that expenditure will be required to meet the obligation.

A list of things the Company has to do to meet the obligation has been prepared and costed. Part of the cost is self-evident from the fee quote prepared by the specialist consultant whom we intend to commission to prepare a detailed report.

Condition 3. A reliable estimate can be made of the expenditure.

The estimates of the costs involved have been prepared in consultation with the independent specialist consultant.

....*(insert name)*

Managing/Finance Director

For and on behalf of the board of

....*(insert name of company)*

....*(insert date)*

Open letter of disclosure

If HMRC has told you it will carry out an inspection of your payroll records in the near future, you may wish to make your own check to make sure everything's in order. If you find any errors what should you do?

How to proceed

You should inform HMRC as soon as possible. Trying to conceal your mistake might well land you in serious trouble. But how should you proceed? The answer is "keep it simple". Use our draft **Open Letter of Disclosure** as your first step to resolving potential conflict with HMRC.

OPEN LETTER OF DISCLOSURE

HMRC

.... *(insert address)*

....

....

....

.... *(insert date)*

Reference:............................. *(insert your company's/business's tax reference)*

Dear Sir

.... *(insert name of business)*

In anticipation of the forthcoming PAYE inspection we have made a thorough review of our business records. Regrettably, we noted an anomaly [some anomalies] and would like to draw this [these] to your attention with a view to settling the unpaid duties as early as possible.

The errors referred to above are set out in detail on the enclosed schedule. We would like to discuss this matter prior to commencement of your inspection. In view of this we would be grateful if you would telephone .... *(insert name of director/partner/member of staff)* at your earliest convenience.

Yours faithfully

.... *(insert signature)*

Enc

Out of time letter

Your involvement in an enquiry usually begins when you receive a letter saying that you are the subject of one and asking you to send further information. However, before you reply you ought to check out whether the enquiry has been made in time.

DELIVERED TOO LATE

The statutory requirement is that a notice of enquiry must be given, i.e. received by the taxpayer within the time allowed. For example, with income tax HMRC has to issue a notice by the anniversary of the date the tax return was received, if it was received on or before the filing date of 31 January (see below if the return was received by HMRC after 31 January). There is a presumption that a notice will be delivered in the ordinary course of post; but this is a rebuttable presumption. What matters is when the notice is actually delivered. If you can show that the notice was delivered after the deadline, it doesn't matter one jot when it was posted; use our **Out of Time Letter** to politely have the enquiry set aside.

Note. If HMRC received the return after 31 January, it has *"up to and including the quarter day next following the first anniversary of the day on which the return was delivered…"* (s.9A(s)(b) of the **Taxes Management Act 1970**) within which to issue the notice of enquiry. The quarter days are 31 January, 30 April, 31 July and 31 October.

OUT OF TIME LETTER

HMRC

....(insert address)

....

....

....

....(insert date)

Dear ....(insert name)

Enquiry notice out of time

....(insert name and tax reference)

Thank you for your enquiry notification dated ......(insert date).

Unfortunately I/we cannot respond to this as the notice itself was delivered outside the time limit for opening such enquiries.

[You can see from the attached photocopy that your notice was date stamped as received by me/us after the deadline for delivering such a notice]

If you have any queries please do not hesitate to contact me/us.

Yours sincerely

....(insert name)

....(insert company name)

Enc

Private expenditure checklist

During a full enquiry by HMRC, if your business records don't stack up, you can expect the inspector to start asking questions about your private expenditure ("the private side"). Their presumption is that any "missing" money would be reflected in a better lifestyle for you. However, you can turn this idea against them with simple summary showing how modest the "private side" is.

A FULL ENQUIRY

If you're subject to a full enquiry into your tax affairs, you may be asked to draw up a list of private expenditure for a year (usually in the current tax year or last accounts tax year). Our **Private Expenditure Checklist** aims to cover the majority of items you should take into account.

PRIVATE EXPENDITURE CHECKLIST

Type of expenditure	£ pw	£ pm	£ pa	Notes
Accommodation				
Rent or mortgage				
Endowment policy				
Mortgage protection				
Council tax				
Water rates and sewerage				
Gas				
Electricity				
Solid fuel				
Buildings insurance				
House contents insurance				
Home telephone				
Home broadband				
Repairs and redecoration				
Major alterations				Extensions/kitchens/bathrooms/double glazing /conservatory/solar panels
Household equipment and fittings				
Kitchen equipment				Cooker/fridge/freezer/dishwasher/washing machine/tumble dryer/microwave
Other electrical equipment				Vacuum cleaner/iron
Crockery, cutlery, glassware				
Carpets and curtains				
Bedding				
Luxury items				Sauna/solarium/billiard room
Garden				
Equipment				Tools/pots/electrical equipment
Repairs and improvements				Shed/patio/greenhouse/barbecue

Type of expenditure	£ pw	£ pm	£ pa	Notes
Garden furniture				
Plants and seeds				Include other consumable, e.g. chemicals
Domestic and other help				
Cleaner				
Window cleaner				
Childminder				Regular babysitters
Gardener				
Food				
Weekly expenditure				Include milk/fresh goods/freezer items
Eating out				
Take away				
Meals at work				
Drinking and entertaining				
Confectionery				
Clothing and personal				
Personal clothing				Work clothing
Children's clothing				School uniforms
Cosmetics, toiletries				
Hairdressing				Manicure/pedicure/massage
Transport				
Car expenses				Capital repayments/insurance/servicing/road tax/rescue services/fuel/repairs
Motorcycles				
Home-to-work travel				Season tickets
Caravan				Annual charges/cleaning/capital items
Health				
Medical insurance (if paid privately)				
Eye tests and glasses				
Dental expenses				
Prescription costs				

Type of expenditure	£ pw	£ pm	£ pa	Notes
Finance and investments				
Income tax and Class 4 NI				
Class 2 NI				
Bank charges and interest				Credit charges/annual fees for credit cards
Life insurance				
Personal pensions				Regular premium/single premium
Premium bonds				
Regular savings				ISAs
Antiques and collectibles				
Jewellery				
Leisure and entertainment				
TV licence				Include licence
Subscription to satellite/cable				Sky/Netflix etc.
Mobile phone				
Mobile broadband				
DVDs				Purchase and rental
Computers				Peripherals/printer/paper/internet costs
Computer software				
Games consoles				Cost of games
Music systems				
CDs, downloads etc.				
Books				
Newspaper and magazines				Regular subscription
Music				Instruments/lessons/music/instrument insurance
Theatre/cinema				
Sport participation				Club membership/equipment/ playing fees
Sport spectating				Season tickets/periodic tickets
Hobbies				Capital and revenue costs
Education				Adult education/Open University

Type of expenditure	£ pw	£ pm	£ pa	Notes
National Lottery				
Gambling				Horses/dogs/football pools/casino
Pets				Food/care
Holidays				
Travel costs				
Accommodation				Timeshare
Spending money				
Gifts and donations				
Presents				Special family events
Charitable giving				
Children and grandchildren				
Schooling				Nursery/school fees/school trips
Extra curricular				Music lessons/coaching/exam fees
Pocket money				
University contributions				
Exam rewards				
Weddings				
Totals				
Total private expenditure per annum	x52	x12		

Product mix reconstruction

When carrying out a business economics exercise, the tax inspector will often use an industry average mark-up of purchases to selling price to construct a sales figure. But this simple calculation doesn't take into account your business's product mix. Use this template to demonstrate that the inspector's calculations are based on flawed assumptions.

ESTABLISH YOUR PRODUCT MIX

As most businesses sell more than one item, the first step in challenging an inspector's business economics exercise is to establish the product mix for your business, i.e. the range of products sold and in what proportion. Do this for a sample period, e.g. three months, and you can generally get this information from a review of sales/purchase invoices. We've set out a **Product Mix Reconstruction** document to help you with this and to provide you with evidence to submit to the tax inspector that their assumptions need upgrading.

PRODUCT MIX RECONSTRUCTION

Reconstruction

We have examined the detailed records of the business for a representative period and arrived at the following factual data about the mix of, and mark-up rates for, the products sold.

Data 1: Total purchases in the period were £78,275.

Data 2: The proportion of each product sold expressed as a percentage of total purchases (100%) is as follows:

Type of product	%
Groceries	25
Cigarettes	45
Confectionary	15
Stationery	15
Total	**100**

Data 3: The mark up on the cost of each product sold for each product type was found to be as follows:

Type of product	Mark up
Groceries	1.18
Cigarettes	1.10
Confectionary	1.25
Stationery	1.13

Our calculation of maximum achievable sales is as follows:

Product type	Purchase cost (*) £	MUR	Expected sales (**) £
Groceries	19,569	1.18	23,091
Cigarettes	35,224	1.10	38,746
Confectionary	11,741	1.25	14,676
Stationery	11,741	1.13	13,267
TOTAL	78,275		89,780

(*) Total purchases (data 1) x product mix percentage (data 2)
(**) Expected sales = purchase cost x mark-up rate (MUR) (data 3)

Conclusion

Our £89,780 is not significantly different from the total sales figure shown in the accounts (£90,000), rather than your overstated figure of £100,000 (£80,000 x 1.25).

Rejecting a business economics exercise

It is possible to reject HMRC's business economics exercise approach completely, if you have reasonable grounds of course. How should you go about this?

ARE YOUR RECORDS DEFICIENT?

HMRC's business economics exercise approach to increase taxable profits cannot be justified unless the records have been shown to be deficient in some way. An inspector should be able to demonstrate that:

(1) There are deficiencies in the records.

(2) The results shown by the accounts are not credible.

(3) Drawings are inadequate.

The fewer of these features present, the more the inspector's decision to base their attack on a business economics exercise should be challenged. So use our **Rejecting a Business Economics Exercise** letter if you want to negotiate this way.

REJECTING A BUSINESS ECONOMICS EXERCISE

....*(insert name)*

HMRC

....*(insert address)*

....

....

....

....*(insert date)*

Dear .... *(insert name)*

....***(insert name and tax reference)***

I/we refer to your letter of ..... *(insert date)*, received on ......*(insert date)* and note your comments.

My/our understanding is that a business economics exercise approach cannot be justified unless the records have been shown to be deficient in some way. You have been unable to demonstrate to my/our satisfaction that: (1) there are deficiencies in the records; (2) the results shown by the accounts are not credible; and (3) the drawings are inadequate. As these features are not present, we challenge the use of any business economics exercise in line with the decision in the Scott t/a Farthings Steak House v McDonald (HMIT) (1996) STC(SCO) 381 (SpC91).

Yours sincerely

....*(insert signature)*

Reply to a business economics exercise

You might feel that the tax demand based on a business economics exercise routine is absolutely outrageous. What measured response should you give?

Don't say too much

During an enquiry into a tax return there is now a much greater willingness by HMRC to displace the profits shown by your accounts with an estimate based on a simple business economics exercise. Using a written **Reply to a Business Economics Exercise**, try to undermine the calculations without showing your hand. Quite often what appear to be "wild" calculations are deliberate in order to get you to say too much.

REPLY TO A BUSINESS ECONOMICS EXERCISE

....*(insert name)*

HMRC

....*(insert address)*

....

....

....

....*(insert date)*

Dear ....*(insert name)*

....**(insert name and tax reference)**

I refer to your letter of ..... *(insert date)* received on ......*(insert date)* and note your comments.

In my/our opinion a business economics exercise cannot prove conclusively what the profits of the business were, based as it is on information supplied some years after the event. The basis of your exercise was to find an expense that had some direct relation to the income of the business. Because the scope for inaccuracies in such an exercise is so vast, I have the following reservations about your calculations not only in terms of the detailed figures used but also of the overall credibility of the ratios used.

(You then go on to attack the HMRC's calculations in detail using our checklist for attacking a business economics exercise.)

I would be grateful if you could include the amended detail in your calculations.

Yours sincerely

....*(insert signature)*

Request for closure letter

If you believe you've given an inspector all the information they've requested, you can ask them to close the enquiry. If they refuse, it might be because they are still on a fishing expedition or won't admit to their boss that they can't hit the targets on this case. What can you do to move things on?

ATTEMPT A NEGOTIATED SETTLEMENT

If the inspector has already dragged out the investigation, you can act, safe in the knowledge that they may be suffering internal pressure to settle one of their (by now) older cases. There is nothing to lose in attempting a negotiated settlement. Use our **Request for Closure Letter** to try and convince HMRC to reconsider closing the enquiry. You can also threaten to have your particular case listed before a tax tribunal and seek to get a closure notice imposed. Even the mention of this to the inspector might make them reconsider their stance.

CONSIDERATIONS

Various factors should be considered before applying to the tribunal for such a closure notice, including:

- the length of time that the enquiry has been on-going
- how co-opertive you have been with HMRC - try to be proactive when responding to an HMRC enquiry
- the manner in which HMRC has conducted the enquiry; and
- the extent of the outstanding queries/requests from HMRC.

REQUEST FOR CLOSURE LETTER

HMRC

....*(insert address)*

....

....

....

....*(insert date)*

Dear ....*(insert name)*

Request for closure of the enquiry (s.28A(4), Taxes Management Act 1970)

....***(insert name and tax reference)***

Further to your last letter ......*(insert date)*.

I/we now believe that I/we have provided you all the information and explanations relevant to the enquiry since it was opened on ..... *(insert date)*.

I/we can see no further advantage for you or me/us in carrying on this enquiry and would ask you to formally close it. If you do not wish to then I/will have to consider having this matter listed before a tax tribunal and seek a Closure Notice.

I/we think it is only fair to let you know that in my/our opinion if, you do wish to keep the enquiry open this might not be seen to be reasonable or defensible should a formal complaint be made by me/ourselves.

Yours sincerely

....*(insert signature)*

Self-employed pages review

Before filing a tax return it's a good idea to carry out last minute health checks with a view to reducing the chance of it being selected for an enquiry. This is especially important if you are self-employed. How can you check that your answers won't raise suspicion?

CHECK YOUR ANSWERS

Before submitting any return you should compare all your answers with a copy of last year's return. Satisfy yourself that you can explain any variances in the figures and if these are substantial, write an explanation in the "additional information" box (otherwise known as the white space). In particular, if you have any self-employed income, it's likely you will need to fill in supplementary pages and include them with your main personal tax return. Checking your answers are consistent with last year's is a good place to start as HMRC's pre-enquiry screening techniques pick up on any variances. In addition, use the questions in our **Self-employed Pages Review** to reduce the chances of being selected for an enquiry.

SELF-EMPLOYED PAGES REVIEW

Section of self-employed pages	Actioned
Business details Are the name and description of the business the same as on last year's return? Does the accounting period follow on from last year's return?	
Business income Make sure you don't include bank interest received in the "Your turnover" box as this may distort your gross profit percentage. This should be included in the "Any other business income" box.	
Turnover below £79,000 If your turnover is under £79,000 for 2013/14, then you can use the short pages and include your total business expenses in the "Total allowable expenses" box rather than separating them out. If your turnover is significantly different from last year then put an explanation in the additional information box. Check that your ratio of net profit to turnover is consistent with last year. If it is higher check that you have not left any expenses out. If it is lower consider making an additional disclosure as to why it has changed. **Note.** If your turnover has been just under £79,000 for the last two years, this could trigger an enquiry. If it has been, then consider using the detailed boxes for over £79,000 (full form) instead.	
Business expenses (turnover over £79,000) You are expected to translate your accounts into entries for boxes in this section. There are probably fewer headings on HMRC's return than are used in your accounts. So you'll need to amalgamate some figures together. For example, there is no separate heading for printing and postage expenses which means you will have to include them under "Phone, fax, stationery and other office costs" (which you should use instead of "Other business expenses" as much as possible). It's a good idea to annotate a copy of the detailed profit and loss account (from your self employed accounts) with the box numbers you have used for each expense heading, and keep this with your copy of the finished tax return. Indeed, are the expenses claimed in the same boxes as last year's return?	

Section of self-employed pages	Actioned
Business expenses (turnover over £79,000) (cont.) Has there been a big increase in the ratio of your purchases to sales, which needs explaining in the additional information box?	
Disallowed expenses HMRC will expect to see some disallowed expenses. In particular: Has an amount for entertainment been disallowed? Has a private use element of expenses been disallowed, e.g. an element of both telephone costs and motor expenses? Has depreciation and loss/profit on sale of assets been disallowed?	
Capital allowances Have you claimed for capital allowances on any vehicles and equipment used in your business (Boxes 23 to 25 (short form) Boxes 49 to 57 (full form)? **Note.** If there is private use of an asset then the figure you claim for capital allowances must be reduced by this before being entered on the form (e.g. 20% private use would mean only 80% of the figure goes on the return).	
Adjustments to arrive at taxable profits If you had an overlap profit carried forward figure (Box 70 (full form)) on last year's return make sure you enter it this year as well so that it doesn't get forgotten. **Note.** Overlap relief can only be claimed in the year you cease self-employment or if you change your accounting date which results in your accounting period being more than twelve months.	
Class 4 NI Check that any Class 4 NI which is payable has been entered in Box 4 of the Tax Calculation summary page.	
Sub-contractors in the construction industry If relevant, remember to enter in Box 38 (short form) or Box 81 (full form) the total amount of tax deducted by contractors shown on the CIS payment summaries that you have.	
Summary balance sheet If you do decide to enter balance sheet figures on SEF (self-employment full) 5 (although it's not compulsory), ask yourself if the drawings figure (in the capital account) is reasonable and consistent	

Section of self-employed pages	Actioned
with your living standards and past year's figures.	
Overall Compare all your answers with a copy of last year's return. Satisfy yourself that you can explain any variances in the figures and if these are substantial write an explanation in the additional information Box 103 (otherwise known as the white space) on page SEF6. If the variations are because of a change of year-end, cessation or commencement then provide full details of the event and any calculations that arose as a result. **Note**. The additional information box will only be read if your case is being considered for enquiry. That's when what you record there could deselect you from further enquiry.	

Wastage/losses record

HMRC typically uses a mark-up of purchases to selling price to construct an anticipated sales figure. However, this doesn't generally allow for wastage/write-offs. So what simple records could you keep about "wastage"?

WASTED STOCK

Product losses can take many forms: discounts and other price reductions made to specific groups of customers or in response to competition; special offers; annual sales; scrappage of stock; wastage arising from spillage, breakage, processing, perishables or inexperience; and pilferage by suppliers (e.g. short measures) or staff.

HMRC may try to argue that your wastage figure is unduly high. However, different businesses in the same sector can have very different levels of wastage. There are many reasons for this, such as misjudging the market and ordering too many perishable goods or, perhaps, a desire to maintain high standards.

Acceptable evidence? Any diary notes kept by you during the year will assist in justifying your reductions for wastage from the maximum figures calculated by HMRC. It can be particularly difficult to justify a figure for wastage in the absence of records. This could be established by keeping details for a sample current period using our **Wastage/Losses Record**.

WASTAGE/LOSSES RECORD

Week 1 *	Product (quantity/units lost)	Customer/member of staff	Estimated value (£)
Discounts			
Price reductions			
Special offers			
Sales			
Scrappage			
Spillage			
Breakage			
Processing			
Perishables			
Inexperience			
Pilferage/theft			
Short supplies			
Total			
Week 2 *			
Discounts			
Price reductions			
Special offers			
Sales			
Scrappage			
Spillage			
Breakage			
Processing			
Perishables			
Inexperience			
Pilferage/theft			
Short supplies			
Total			

Note

* *If there is a monthly cycle to the business then it's best to keep a record for four weeks. If it's a quarterly cycle consider keeping a record for three months.*

What HMRC is likely to ask

There's a pretty standard set of questions that the inspector will ask at interview. These are mostly designed to undermine the records you've kept and so allow them to make a demand for tax on missing income/profits or over-claimed expenses. So how should you prepare for such an interview?

GUIDELINES

If you attend an interview, the inspector should start by explaining that they will ask questions and take notes on your answers. It's best to answer all questions truthfully but not to elaborate. If the inspector wants the detail they can ask. Use our guide to **What HMRC is Likely to Ask** to help prepare for your interview.

WHAT HMRC IS LIKELY TO ASK

The business

The inspector will know the trade (e.g. taxi driver, public house) but they do not know the particular facets of your business (e.g. for a pub is food sold or is it largely beer sales?). The purpose of the questioning will be to try and ascertain a picture of the trade carried on. Remember, you know far more about the business than they do.

Record keeping

The inspector will generally, after the interview, ask to have all the business records for review. They need, therefore, to understand your record keeping and will ask such questions as: What books are maintained? Who writes them up? How often is this done?

Your accountant's work

Next to be reviewed will be the work undertaken by your accountant. They will want to know, if not covered in the opening letter, what estimates were used, what balance was necessary to square the cash account and how the accountant dealt with that. They will also cover the adjustments necessary to arrive at taxable profit from the profit shown in your accounts, e.g. an adjustment for private use of a motor vehicle.

Drawings and private expenditure

In order that the inspector can confirm whether the profits are sufficient to meet the capital expenditure and personal and private expenditure, they will review the drawings from the business and your personal needs. They will want to know what is spent in cash, e.g. housekeeping, private spending, whether holidays have been taken and whether you have any hobbies, i.e. what do you spend your money on?

Assets

If the inspector has not already asked you to complete a Statement of Assets, they will try to establish the investments held and assets purchased (particularly properties). What did it cost? How much of it was financed? Do you have an outstanding loan balance? Have you lent monies to family and friends that haven't been repaid? Have you extended your home? What did it cost and how was it financed?

Other monies received

Do you gamble? Have sums been received by way of a loan? Any legacies? This is to stop the items being offered as excuses once the extent of any understatement of income has been calculated.

Section 4

Elections and claims

Allocation of savings interest agreement

If spouses or civil partners do not want a 50/50 split of savings interest, they can declare that income be split according to each person's beneficial entitlement as detailed in a written agreement.

BENEFICIAL OWNERSHIP OF BANK ACCOUNT FUNDS

As a general rule, assets owned by spouses in joint names are treated by HMRC as shared equally by both partners, and any income produced will be taxed accordingly. But where actual ownership of an asset differs from 50/50, a married couple or civil partnership can elect to be taxed on their actual share of any income it produces.

However, until 2011 HMRC would not accept an election for unequal ownership in respect of bank accounts. Its view was that any interest a joint account produced must be declared and taxed on a 50/50 basis because the money in joint accounts is equally accessible to both spouses.

In practice, where both spouses pay in and withdraw money from an account, it can be virtually impossible to say how much of the balance belongs to each. This means it's also impossible to say how much interest each is entitled to. This problem can be overcome by spouses agreeing how much money in an account belongs to each of them.

Use our **Allocation of Savings Interest Agreement** to indicate who is the beneficial owner of the money in your joint bank accounts and thus the extent to which interest is taxable on each of you.

NOTIFYING HMRC

Once you've made the agreement, send a copy of it with a **Form 17** election to notify HMRC how the interest is to be allocated for tax purposes. A Form 17 can be viewed and downloaded from the HMRC website (http://www.hmrc.gov.uk/forms/form17.pdf).

TIME LIMIT

A Form 17 must be sent to HMRC within 60 days of the date of declaration. This deadline will not be extended for any reason.

ALLOCATION OF SAVINGS INTEREST AGREEMENT

Bank account ………….. *(e.g. number 01234568)*

…………… and …………… *(insert names)* are the joint legal and beneficial owners of the above named savings account (the account) and, in accordance with the terms and conditions of the operation of the account as set out and varied from time to time by the bank, have equal and several rights over the money in it.

…………. and …………… *(insert names)* both contribute money to and withdraw money from the account. While recognising this ……….. and ………….. *(insert names)* agree that from the date of this agreement the money held in the account at any time shall be beneficially owned as follows:

- …………. *(insert name)* 20%
- …………. *(insert name)* 80%

Interest

All interest paid or accrued in respect of money held in the account will be due to …………. and …………. *(insert names)* in proportion to their respective beneficial ownership as determined by this agreement.

Signature ……………………….. Name …………………… Date ……………

Signature ……………………….. Name …………………… Date ……………

Witness:

Signature ……………………….. Name …………………… Date ……………

Address…………………………………………………………………………….

Election to change a pension input period

Tax relief for contributions to registered pension schemes is limited to an annual maximum, which is currently £40,000. However, the contributions to be taken into account for this calculation are not those paid during the same tax year, but all those paid to schemes which have a pension input period (PIP) ending in the same tax year. As each pension scheme can have a different PIP this can make the calculation tricky.

HOW AND WHEN TO USE THIS ELECTION

You can simplify matters by changing the PIP for one or more of your pension schemes. Although there's no requirement for you to notify HMRC of this election, it's important you keep a record of it for your tax records.

The request to change a PIP must be sent to the pension scheme administrator, e.g. the insurance company with which the pension plan is held. Only one change of PIP per tax year may be made.

Use our draft request to notify the pension company of a change to a PIP.

ELECTION TO CHANGE A PENSION INPUT PERIOD

ABC Mutual Life Assurance (example)
....*(insert address)*
....
....
....

....*(insert date)*

Dear Sirs

....***(insert your name)***

....***(insert your pension plan reference number)***

Please accept this letter as a request to amend the pension input period (PIP) end date to ....*(insert date, e.g. 5 April each year)* for the above named scheme with effect for the next PIP commencing after the current one ends.

Please send me confirmation when this request has been effected.

Yours faithfully

....*(insert signature)*

In-year pension contribution - claim for tax relief

Use our form, which you can adapt to fit your situation, to obtain tax relief for your pension contributions by an adjustment to your tax code.

WHEN TO USE THIS FORM

If you pay contributions to a:

- pension plan, e.g. a personal pension plan, and pay tax at the higher (40%) or additional (45%) rates; or

- retirement annuity contract - that's a pension plan started prior to June 1988, and pay tax at any rate

you are entitled to claim a reduction in your tax liability.

Tax relief for pension contributions must be claimed on your self-assessment tax return. However, where you make a one-off additional pension contribution, or increase your regular contributions, leaving your claim until you complete and submit your tax return can mean you have to wait much longer to receive tax relief; almost two years from the date of the contribution wouldn't be unusual. But if you pay tax through the PAYE system you can receive the tax relief earlier by making an in-year claim.

IN-YEAR PENSION CONTRIBUTION - CLAIM FOR TAX RELIEF

HMRC
.... *(insert address)*
....
....
....

.... *(insert date)*

Dear Sirs

.... ***(insert your name)***

.... ***(insert your ten digit tax reference)***

On .... *(insert date)* I made a contribution of £.......... *(insert amount)* net, equating to £.......... gross, to my pension plan with .... *(insert name of insurance company etc.)*. My total gross pension contributions for the current tax year will therefore be £.............. *(insert amount)*.

Please amend my tax code to take account of the higher rate tax relief due on my total pension payments.

Yours faithfully

.... *(insert signature)*

Letter to chase a tax repayment

Repayments arising from online filing of self assessment tax returns may be stopped for a variety of reasons, and HMRC staff have to look at them before they can be released. Contacting HMRC should help to speed up your repayment.

WRITE OR PHONE?

Telephone contact is often the quickest way to get things done, as you might get a response straight away. If you do phone, it's a good idea to make a note of the name of the person you speak to.

However, you may prefer to send a **Letter to Chase a Tax Repayment**. If you do, always show your tax office reference. Keep a copy of your letter and any other papers sent in case the original goes astray. If you write to your tax office, you might wait some weeks for a reply; you can check by when you are likely to receive a reply by using HMRC's Where's My Reply? tool (http://www.hmrc. gov.uk/tools/progress-tool/index.htm) and selecting Self Assessment.

LETTER TO CHASE A TAX REPAYMENT

HMRC

....*(insert address)*

....

....

....

....*(insert date)*

Dear ....*(insert name)*

Subject: Outstanding Tax Repayment

Name: .... *(insert your name)*

UTR: .... *(insert the ten digit unique tax reference on the return)*

NI number: .... *(insert your NI number)*

With reference to my self-assessment tax return for ..... *(insert e.g. 2013/14)*, submitted on ......*(insert date)*, I am surprised that I have not yet received the tax repayment claimed.

This letter is to formally ask you to expedite matters and I should be grateful if you would issue the repayment cheque/transfer the funds to my account *[delete as necessary]* as soon as possible.

I would be grateful if you could acknowledge receipt of this letter and its contents.

Yours sincerely

....*(insert signature)*

Official error ESC A19 claim

If HMRC has delayed using information in its possession and this results in you paying too little tax, it can write off the arrears of tax under extra-statutory concession (ESC) A19. However, despite being fully aware of this concession, you may need to "remind" HMRC of it in writing.

EXTRA-STATUTORY CONCESSION A19

In tax law there is a little known concession (ESC A19) which protects the taxpayer where HMRC demands past taxes but where delay by HMRC makes it unfair for them to be collected. For example, where you told HMRC about other income to include in your tax code, but it ignored it. Tax arrears can be written of if three conditions are met:

1. HMRC failed to make "*proper and timely*" use of the information provided to it

2. the taxpayer "could reasonably have believed that their affairs were in order"

3. no notification was sent to the taxpayer within twelve months of the end of the tax year in question.

RESISTANCE FROM HMRC

Unfortunately, HMRC routinely ignores this concession, even if the conditions are met, and will often send a tax demand with no mention of the concession. Use our **Official Error ESCA19 Claim** letter to appeal against the tax demand. If HMRC still resists, take the complaint to the Tax Adjudicator.

OFFICIAL ERROR ESC A19 CLAIM

HMRC

....(*insert address*)

....

....

....

....(*insert date*)

Dear ....(*insert name*)

Arrears of tax due to official error ESC A19 claim

....(***insert name***)

....(***insert NI number***)

....(***insert any other reference shown on the P800***)

I have received your tax calculation for the tax year[s]......... (*insert the tax year that applies to you*).

The calculation suggests that I have underpaid tax for......(*insert the tax year or years*).

I was unaware that my tax affairs were not in order. I had thought that all the tax that I was due to pay was deducted under PAYE. I believe that the underpayment has arisen because you failed to take action upon relevant information already in your possession for the year[s] in question.

For the tax year.......... I appreciate that you are not notifying me of the arrears more than twelve months after the end of the tax year in which you received the information indicating that more tax was due. However, I feel that the "exceptional circumstances" condition applies because you:

• failed more than once to make proper use of the facts you had been given about my sources of income

• allowed the arrears to build up over two whole tax years in succession by failing to make proper and timely use of information that you had been given.

I am therefore requesting that under the provisions of ESC A19 that the whole of the underpayment as shown on the P800 should be remitted.

I look forward to hearing from you.

Yours sincerely

....*(insert signature)*

Overpayment relief claim checksheet

Where you make a mistake in your individual, company or partnership, tax return and the time limit for correcting this under the self-assessment rules has passed, you can submit an "overpayment claim" to recover any tax overpaid. But HMRC isn't obliged to accept every claim.

WHAT ARE THE RULES?

There are tough rules which specify the circumstances in which HMRC won't refund tax overpaid. Our **Overpayment Relief Claim Checksheet** sets them out, saving you time and effort in deciding whether they apply.

OVERPAYMENT RELIEF CLAIM CHECKSHEET

There are a several situations where HMRC is not bound to allow an overpayment claim. These are specified in **Para 2 Schedule 1AB Taxes Management Act 1970** as relating to overpayments arising:

- Case A -
  - from a mistake in any other claim, election or notice, e.g. accidentally claiming a tax relief for the wrong year; or
  - because of a failure to make a claim, election or notice; or
  - from a mistake in allocating expenditure to a capital allowances pool, or failing to do so; or
  - because of a failure to bring into account the disposal value of an asset for capital allowances

- Case B - where a claim can be made to achieve the same result under rules and legislation, e.g. where a repayment can be made by amending a tax return

- Case C - where the tax relief was subject to a time limit and the claimant didn't take steps to make the claim within this, and they knew, or ought to have known, to do so

- Case D - where the reason for the claim has been the subject of a case considered by a court or tribunal or has been the subject of an appeal to HMRC settled without reference to a court or tribunal

- Case E - where the person knew, or should have known, they had grounds to make a claim for repayment but failed to do so before the later of:

  - the date an appeal relating to the amount overpaid was settled (this includes where the taxpayer withdrew their appeal) in a court or tribunal, but the reason now given for the overpayment wasn't mentioned as part of the case; and
  - the date by which they had the right to make an appeal

- Case F - where the tax in question has been collected, or is due to be collected, under enforcement proceedings by HMRC, or under an agreement aimed at avoiding such proceedings

- Case G - as a result of a mistake in the calculation of a person's tax liability (except a PAYE calculation), where this was made in accordance with the generally accepted practice at the time

- Case H - as a result of a mistake in PAYE assessment or calculation, where this has been made in accordance with the generally accepted practice as it stood at the end of the twelve months following the end of the tax year for which the assessment or calculation was made.

Overpayment relief claim

Whether you're an individual, company director or partner in a business, where you discover a mistake in your tax return and it's too late to correct under the self-assessment rules, you can make an "overpayment relief claim".

LETTER TO HMRC

This claim needs to be made in writing and include certain information (or HMRC will reject it).

Our draft **Overpayment Relief Claim** guides you through all the information you must include to ensure that your claim is valid.

TIME LIMIT

An overpayment claim may not be made more than four years after the end of the relevant tax year.

OVERPAYMENT RELIEF CLAIM

HMRC

....*(insert address)*

....

....

....

....*(insert date)*

Dear Sir

Overpayment relief claim under (Schedule 1AB TMA 1970) *(if claim relates to income tax or CGT)* **(Paragraph 51 Schedule 18 FA 1998)** *(if claim relates to corporation tax)*

....***(insert your company or partnership name and reference)***

Please accept this letter as a claim for repayment of ………….. *(insert amount of tax overpaid)* being *(income tax/capital gains tax/Class 4 NI)* for the year ended 5 April ……… *(insert year)* in accordance with schedule 1AB Taxes Management Act 1970.

[Or for a claim in respect of corporation tax

Please accept this letter as a claim for repayment of corporation tax of …………… *(insert amount of tax overpaid)* for the accounting period in accordance with Paragraph 51 Schedule 18 Finance Act 1998.]

- I confirm that I am the person *[(or in the case of a company or partnership:)* I am authorised to represent the company/partnership ……….. *(insert name)* which is] entitled to the overpayment relief relating to this claim *[(or in the case of partnerships:)* I am the person nominated by all of the relevant partners *(i.e. all those who were partners any time during the tax year concerned)]*

- I consider that I *(or state the name of the company or partners)* have overpaid tax for the year mentioned above because ………………………… *(state reason for overpayment, e.g. unclaimed tax relief, overstated income etc.; for example "I understated the deduction due in my business accounts for the year ended 5 April 2009 in respect of motor travel". State the amount under claimed etc.)*

- I *(or state the name of the company or partners)* have/have not *(delete as appropriate)* previously claimed or made an appeal in connection to the tax payment/assessment *(delete as appropriate)* in question. *(Where an appeal was made state the date and reason it was made).*

- I enclose evidence that the tax now being reclaimed was paid by me *(or the company or partner). (Attach evidence; this might be for example, a P60, a company or personal self-assessment statement of account etc.)*

- I confirm that the information given in this claim and any documents included with it are, to the best of my knowledge and belief, correct and complete.

Yours faithfully

……………………………… *(insert signature)* ………………………………*(print name)*

(If the claim is being made by a company state the capacity in which you are signing, e.g. "Director". Where the claim relates to a mistake or omission from a partnership tax return it should be signed by a nominated partner, in which case show "Partner" here.)

Pension input period record

Tax relief is limited to pension contributions within the annual allowance.

WHEN TO USE THIS FORM

For the purpose of working out whether the annual allowances has been exceeded, the total contributions are worked out by adding up all the sums paid in the pension input periods (PIPs) ending in the tax year.

A member of a pension scheme can elect to change the PIP and so can the scheme manager, e.g. the insurance company who operates the pension. But only one election can be made per tax year and the first election takes precedence.

The PIP record sheet will help you keep track of the PIPs for each pension scheme you have.

PENSION INPUT PERIOD RECORD

Scheme name	Policy number	Original PIP end date	Change requested on	First new PIP end
ABC Mutual pension plan	*1234567-A*	*15 June*	*1 June 2011*	*5 April 2012*

Purchase of own shares clearance letter

For unquoted trading companies, the amount received by a shareholder on selling their shares back to the company may be treated as capital rather than as a distribution provided certain conditions are met. To prevent any nasty surpirses later on, you can apply for advance clearance to determine the correct treatment.

CONDITIONS

A company share buy-back is a useful way for director shareholders to exit a company. It's usually better for the departing shareholder if the sale qualifies as a capital disposal - particularly if they can take advantage of the 10% entrepreneurs' relief tax rate. But for capital treatment to apply, there are strict conditions set out in s.1033 of the **Corporation Tax Act 2010**. The company must be an unquoted trading company and the repurchase must meet either Condition A or Condition B:

Condition A (all must be met)

- the repurchase is made wholly or mainly in order to benefit the trade carried on by the company (or a 75% subsidiary). For example, a long-standing director wishing to depart to allow new younger management to take the company forward would be to the benefit of the trade.

- the repurchase does not form part of a scheme or arrangement which aims either to enable the participation in the profits of the company without receiving a dividend or for the avoidance of tax

- the seller must be UK resident in the tax year of the purchase

- the seller must have owned the shares for at least five years (three years if acquired as a result of a death, and the ownership period of the deceased is included). Holding periods of a spouse are aggregated for this purpose.

- there must be a substantial reduction in the vendor's shareholding - the fraction after the buy-back must not exceed 75% of the fraction beforehand

- following the buy-back the seller must not be connected with the company.

or

Condition B

- the whole, or substantially the whole, of the payment is to provide funds to pay a person's IHT bill within the period of two years after the death.

ADVANCE CLEARANCE

To avoid uncertainty as to whether the capital treatment will apply to your company's share repurchase, you can apply to HMRC for advance clearance. Use our **Purchase of Own Shares Clearance Letter** to do this.

PURCHASE OF OWN SHARES CLEARANCE LETTER

HM Revenue & Customs
CA Clearance SO528
PO Box 194
Bootle
L69 9AA

……………….. *(insert date)*

Dear Sirs

……………….. ***(insert your company name)***
Section 1033 Corporation Tax Act 2010 Clearance - purchase of own shares

We are writing to apply for advance clearance under s.1044 Corporation Tax Act 2010 in respect of a proposed share buy-back by ……………….. *(insert your company name)*.

Unless otherwise stated, statutory references in this letter refer to the Corporation Tax Act 2010.

The shares are to be repurchased from ……………….. *(insert shareholder's name)*.

In accordance with HMRC's Statement of Practice 2/82, we provide the following information which is relevant to your consideration of whether the share buy-back is regarded as qualifying to be treated as capital under s.1033.

1. The company

1.1 [Details of company registration number, unique taxpayer reference and tax office]

1.2 [Outline of company's activities]

2. The group *(if applicable)*

2.1 [Names of subsidiaries, unique taxpayer references and percentage held]

3. The Shareholders

3.1 The current shareholders of the Company are as follows [Amend as appropriate for different classes of shares]

Name	Ordinary shares
[Shareholder]	[Number]

[Total]

3.2 [Outline rights attaching to shares]

3.3 [Other relevant details ie. any relationships between shareholders]

4. The business

4.1 The Company's trading results over the last three financial years are detailed below:-

	[Accounting period]	[Accounting period]	[Accounting period]
Profit before tax (£)			
Tax charge (£)			
Profit after tax (£)			

5. The proposed transaction

5.1 [Outline proposed transaction and payment to be received by shareholder]

5.2 [How is proposed transaction to be funded]

5.3 [Other relevant information]

6. Purpose and benefits

6.1 [Explain the reason for the proposed transaction]

7. Section 1033(2)

7.1 We confirm that the proposed purchase does not form part of a scheme or arrangement the main purposes of which is to enable any individual to participate in the profits of the Company without receiving a dividend, or the avoidance of tax.

8. Conditions in sections 1034-1043

8.1 [Shareholder] is resident and ordinarily resident in the UK.

8.2 [Shareholder's] tax affairs are dealt with by [Name] Tax office, under the tax reference [xxxxx xxxxx].

8.3 [Shareholder's] holding of x shares was acquired on [date/s], and as such the Company considers that the ownership period requirement in s.1035 is fulfilled.

8.4 The vendor's interest in the Company will be substantially reduced for the purposes of s.1037 because [all of his shares will be repurchased] [or] [as follows:]

8.5 [Calculation of interest before and after transaction as presented in s.1037]

8.6 We can confirm that under the provisions of s.1042, [Shareholder] will not be connected with the Company or its subsidiaries immediately after the purchase.

8.7 [Shareholder] has no outstanding loans with the Company.

9. Accounts and other financial information

9.1 Please find enclosed a copy of the most recent consolidated accounts for the period ended [Date]. The Company is not aware of any materially relevant changes since the balance sheet date.

10. Clearances sought

10.1 We trust that the above information is sufficient, and should be grateful to receive confirmation from the Board of H M Revenue and Customs that s.1033 will apply to treat the entire proceeds of the as a repayment of capital.

Yours faithfully

……………….. *(insert name)*

……………….. *(insert position in company)*

Purchase of own shares reporting letter

Regardless of whether you have applied for advance clearance, where capital treatment has been applied to a share buy-back, you must report the transaction to HMRC.

REPORTING TO HMRC

Once a share buy-back has taken place and capital treatment has been applied, the company is required to make a return of information to HMRC within 60 days. There is no HMRC form to complete for this, it simply needs to be a letter addressed to the local office - i.e. the office that deals with the corporation tax affairs of the company. This must give details of the payment and the reasons for treating the transaction as capital rather than a distribution.

PURCHASE OF OWN SHARES REPORTING LETTER

HMRC

………………………… *(insert tax office address)*

……………………….

……………………….

……………………….

……………………….

Date: ………………………… *(insert date)*

Dear Sirs

………………………….*(insert your company name)*

UTR……………………..*(insert your company's tax reference number)*

Notification of purchase of own shares under section 1,046 Corporation Tax Act 2010

We are writing to notify you that a proposed share buy-back by ……………*(insert your company name)* from ………….. *(insert shareholder's name)* has been effected.

The shares were repurchased on……. *(insert date)* for a cash consideration of [£x].

The company is treating the payment as one to which s.1,033 of the Corporation Tax Act 2010 applies by virtue of the clearance obtained from HMRC, which we attach for your information. We trust that no further information is required. No changes were subsequently made to the proposed transaction detailed in our letter dated …………. *(insert date).*

Yours faithfully

…………………… *(insert your name)*

………………………*(insert your position)*

Short-life asset election

Tax relief on the cost of equipment you buy for your business is spread over decades unless your purchases are covered by the annual investment allowance. The good news is you can accelerate this dramatically with a simple election.

WHEN CAN YOU USE AN ELECTION?

Businesses are allowed tax relief for the cost of machinery and equipment. Each purchase is added to a pool of expenditure and a writing down allowance (WDA) of either 18% or 8%, depending on the type of equipment, allowed on the balance. This means you'll be claiming WDAs on the cost of equipment for many years after it has been scrapped or sold.

To speed up tax relief for certain types of equipment (cars are excluded) you expect to keep for eight or fewer years, you can, instead of pooling the cost, elect to have WDAs worked out for each purchase or class of purchases separately. This is called a **Short-Life Asset Election**. When you sell or scrap the equipment within eight years, you'll be entitled to tax relief for the balance of any of cost (see example).

Note. Where the total expenditure on equipment etc. is less than the annual investment allowance (AIA), a 100% tax deduction can be claimed for this in the financial year in which the purchase is made and therefore an election isn't needed.

EXAMPLE

On 31 May 2013 Acom purchases a file server for £6,000. It has used its AIA against other expenditure in the same financial year. Acom makes an election for the server which it submits to HMRC with its accounts for the financial year to 31 December 2013. It sells the server on 31 August 2015 for £1,000. The tax allowances it claims are as follows:

Year ended 31 December 2013

Qualifying expenditure	£6,000
WDA 2013 - 18%	(£1,080)
Written down value (WDV)	£4,920

Year ended 31 December 2014

WDA 2014 - 18%	(£ 886)
Written down value (WDV)	£4,034

Year ended 31 December 2015

Sold	(£1,000)
Balancing tax allowance	£3,034

SHORT-LIFE ASSET ELECTION

HMRC

.... *(insert address)*

....

....

....

....

Date: .... *(insert date)*

Reference: (*insert your/your company's tax reference*)

Dear Sir

.... *(insert name of business)*

Please accept this letter as an election for short-life asset treatment under the provisions of s.85 Capital Allowances Act 2001. A list of the assets for which this treatment is to apply is set out below [and continued on the attached schedule*].

Yours faithfully

....

[Director, Partner, Proprietor*]

*(*delete as required)*

Date asset purchased	Cost of asset	Description

Section 5

Employee benefits and expenses

Alternative interest calculation method letter

In the case of low or interest-free loans there's more than one way to work out the taxable benefit figure to declare on your P11D. This means you can elect to substitute the figure calculated using the normal average method for the alternative precise one if it's to your advantage. This is where our handy draft election can help.

Two methods

1. **Average loan balance.** Where the interest payable by you on a loan from your company is less than the amount that you would pay at the official rate set by HMRC (3.25% for 2014/15), the difference is a taxable benefit in kind. Usually, interest at the official rate is worked out on the average loan balance. The average balance is arrived at by adding together the amount of the loan outstanding at the beginning of the tax year and the balance at the end of the tax year.

2. **Alternative precise method.** However, if the loan balance varies widely during the year, you could save tax by electing for the "alternative method of calculation". The effect of this is that the official interest is calculated by applying the official rate to the balance of the loan outstanding on each day during the tax year instead of the average. Where your company loan balance has changed because of irregular repayments or advances during the tax year, it's worth checking whether the alternative method can save you tax. But make sure the election is made in time; it must be received by HMRC within twelve months from the 31 January that follows the end of the tax year for which you wish the alternative method to apply, e.g. for 2014/15 the deadline is 31 January 2017.

ALTERNATIVE INTEREST CALCULATION METHOD LETTER

HMRC
....*(insert your tax office)*
....*(insert address)*
....
....

....*(insert date)*

Dear Sirs

Alternative interest method for...*(insert tax year)*

Name: ....*(insert your name)*

UTR: .... *(insert the ten-digit unique tax reference on the return)*

NI number: .... *(insert your NI number)*

Please accept this letter as a notice of election to adopt the alternative interest calculation in respect of the loan(s) made to me by my employer for the above year.

This election is made in accordance with s.183(1)(a) of the Income Tax (Earnings and Pensions) Act 2003.

Yours faithfully

.... *(insert signature)*

Assets with personal use

Where an asset is loaned to an employee there is usually a taxable benefit to declare. This document deals with assets (other than cars, vans, mobile phones or living accommodation) owned by you as an employer but made available for private use by an employee.

RECORD YOUR ASSETS

Where an employee is provided with a company asset which they can use, either partly or completely, for a private purpose, e.g. a digital camera, its annual asset value needs to be reported on form P11D. For most assets, the annual value is 20% of market value (or the rent or hire charge paid if this is greater) when it was first provided to the employee plus running costs you pay for. So in order for you to be able to calculate the amount to include on the P11D, use the **Assets with Personal Use** form and keep a print out of this as a record of the calculation. You will also need to record any amounts that the employee has reimbursed as these will reduce the benefit charge.

ASSETS WITH PERSONAL USE

Employee name: ▭

Employee NI number: ▭

Details of asset provided:

Description: ▭

Original cost/market value: ▭

OR, if paid, hire charge if greater than original cost/market value

Calculation of annual value:

Greater of:

(a) 20% of market value when first made available ▭

(b) rent or hire charges if paid where the asset is not owned ▭

Annual value £ -

Add: annual running costs (e.g. insurance) ▭

Total amount chargeable to tax £ -

Less: amount made good by employee ▭

Amount to enter on P11D £ -

Dispensation renewal letter

Having a dispensation from HMRC means that you don't have to waste time completing P11Ds each year. However, although these technically last indefinitely, HMRC reviews them about every five years to make sure the conditions still apply. How can you make sure that yours is renewed without any problems?

WHY DO YOU NEED A DISPENSATION?

If you have a number of employees, then the preparation of P11Ds can often be time consuming. To reduce the time spent completing them, it's advisable to have a dispensation in place. This is HMRC's agreement that certain business expenses do not need to be reported on Forms P11D, there are no taxable benefits arising and therefore there is nothing to include in the employees' tax codes. There is also no need to pay any employers' NI on items covered by a dispensation.

When dispensations are granted by HMRC, you have to make an application (Form P11DX) and supply various pieces of information about your expense claiming and authorisation procedures. The same applies for renewals. So when HMRC contacts you about reviewing your existing one, use our **Dispensation Renewal Letter** to avoid any delays in this taking place.

DISPENSATION RENEWAL LETTER

HMRC
Local Compliance
Specialist Employer Compliance
…………………………………………………… *(insert address)*
……………………………………………………
……………………………………………………
……………………………………………………
……………………………………………………

…………………………………………………… *(insert date)*

Your reference: ……………………………………….

Dear Sir or Madam

Review of Dispensation

Thank you for your letter dated ………….……. *(insert date)* concerning our existing Dispensation Notice issued to us on …………………….. *(insert date)*.

Please accept this letter as confirmation that the terms of the dispensation are still needed.

To help with your routine checks, please find attached a completed Form P11DX.

Also enclosed is a copy of an employee's completed expense claim [from last month/for the most recent period] *(delete as applicable)* that has been approved for payment.

We would like to revise the existing dispensation by adding the following items, which have been included on the part(s) of the P11DX headed:

> 1. <u>Fees and subscriptions to professional bodies.</u> *(Insert details, e.g. The Institute of Chartered Accountants in England and Wales.)*

> 2. <u>Other expenses.</u> *(Insert details, e.g., mileage payments for employees using their own cars for business purposes and paid within the HMRC authorised rates.)*

Yours faithfully

…………………………………………………… *(insert name)*

…………………………………………………… *(insert position)*

Encs

Electronic devices policy

When removing the Home Computer Initiative back in 2006, HMRC accidentally opened the door to charging tax on private use of any electronic device, such as a laptop or tablet, provided to employees by their company. How can you prevent a tax charge from arising?

COMPUTER-RELATED EQUIPMENT

Tablets and laptops come within the normal rules for computers. HMRC's guidance says that for computers provided to employees by their company to be exempt from benefit-in-kind charges, *"the sole reason the computer must have been provided must be for the individual to carry out their duties of employment"* and that private use must be insignificant.

This means the company must be buying the iPad or laptop principally for business purposes, and that it's required for you or your employee to be able to perform their duties. Greater productivity when commuting, note taking in meetings and performing presentations are all likely to be accepted as valid business reasons.

The definition of insignificant private use can be more problematic however, the latest guidance from HMRC is that the level of an employee's private usage of computer-related equipment provided by their company will not be the deciding factor in whether or not a tax charge arises. If it's made available in order to carry out their duties in the first place, then they are unlikely to be taxed on its private use. So to be able to prove this to HMRC it's best to have an **Electronic Devices Policy** governing the issue (and private use) of each device.

ELECTRONIC DEVICES POLICY

1. Electronic devices are provided by ....*(insert company name)* to enable you to work efficiently and communicate effectively for business purposes.

2. Electronic devices are anything designed to be used, connected to, or inserted into a computer, including printers, scanners, modems, MP3 players and mobile phones with e-mail and Internet access.

3. You must comply with the Company's e-mail and Internet policies at all times, and any breach of them will be regarded as a disciplinary matter.

4. The Company reserves the right to monitor your usage of electronic devices, e-mail and the Internet.

5. We have introduced this policy to ensure that:

    5.1   you make efficient and proper use of IT and communications facilities

    5.2   you do not put our computer systems at risk

    5.3   we are protected from external intrusion

    5.4   our image is properly protected

    5.5   you are aware of what constitutes abuse of these facilities.

6. This policy will be reviewed and updated.

7. Insignificant use of the Company's e-mail facility for personal purposes is permitted. For more information on how the Company defines "insignificant" see ....*(insert contact name)*.

8. Insignificant use of the Company's Internet connection for personal purposes is permitted. For more information on how the Company defines "insignificant", see ....*(insert contact name)*.

9. You are responsible for the security of your electronic devices and must not allow them to be used by any unauthorised person. You should keep your passwords confidential and change them regularly. When leaving your computer unattended, or on leaving the office, you should make sure that you log off to prevent access in your absence.

Expenses claim form

You have an obligation to provide certain information regarding benefits and expenses to HMRC and to your employees. However, it's not always enough to just collect the information - you also need documentation to support the benefit or expense. A good place to start is an expenses claim form.

THE NEED TO KEEP RECORDS

At the end of each tax year, you need to prepare P11D forms for all directors plus employees earning more than £8,500 a year. Collecting and analysing the information for these forms can be an onerous task, and the cost of getting it wrong is potentially very high penalties.

Each employee who claims business expenses over the year should keep all their receipts which match the figures entered on the **Expenses Claim Form**. The procedures for submitting and authorising expense claims should be well documented and communicated to employees.

DISPENSATIONS

Analysing a year's worth of your employees' expense claim forms is a very time-consuming, but necessary, task in order to accurately complete the P11Ds (unless you have a dispensation in place). To apply for a dispensation, you need to complete the Taxman's Form P11DX which can be downloaded at http://www.hmrc.gov.uk/forms/p11dx.pdf. Once you've sent off the initial application, HMRC will usually ask for a copy of your claim form.

EXPENSES CLAIM FORM

Date:

Expense claim reference:

Employee's name:

Department:

Note: Claims should be supported by a VAT receipt/invoice were appropriate

Date DD/MM/YY	Description	Total expense £	VAT included £	Mileage (complete separate claim form)	Other travel £	Meals £	Hotel etc £	Entertaining £	Other £
Total:		0.00	0.00	0.00	0.00	0.00	0.00	0.00	0.00

Signed by:

Authorised by:

Expenses policy

In order to a get a reporting dispensation from HMRC, your procedures for the submission and authorisation of expense claims needs to be well documented and communicated to employees.

EVIDENCE OF A LEGITIMATE CLAIM

In addition to the claim form, HMRC will also ask for a copy of your **Expenses Policy**. It will grant a dispensation if it's happy that no tax will be payable by the employees on the expenses or benefits provided. HMRC wants to know that you have a good system in place to ensure that only business expenses are being reimbursed before agreeing to a dispensation. Therefore, our policy covers all the rules and requirements for legitimate claims, such as prior authorisation and provision of VAT receipts. HMRC will also want to see that the expense claims are always authorised by someone other than the claimant.

EXPENSES POLICY

It is the Company's policy to reimburse employees for all necessary travel, accommodation and other expenses, including the entertainment of clients, incurred while engaged on authorised Company business.

The Company will set levels of expenditure that are deemed appropriate and which may only be varied at the discretion of the Company.

The level of reimbursement allowed will be sufficient to provide a standard and quality which will adequately meet the needs of employees from the viewpoint of both comfort and acceptability for the effective conduct of Company business.

1. The rate of reimbursement is set at levels contained in the attached schedule and may only be varied at the discretion of .... *(insert name).*

2. All expenditure must be authorised by ......*(insert name)* before it is incurred, to ensure that it is both necessarily incurred and reasonable.

3. Employees are expected to obtain valid VAT receipts covering their expenditure; without these, reimbursement may not be made.

4. Employees are required to apply for reimbursement by way of a written claim to .... *(insert name)* on a weekly/monthly* basis.

5. [Advances for anticipated expenditure may be applied for in the same way and must be accounted for properly.] *

6. [Authorised employees who are required to entertain clients regularly on behalf of the Company or otherwise to incur expenses on the Company's behalf will be afforded the facilities for such expenditure, in the form of a credit card. Expenditure will remain subject to the specified Company limits and credit/charge card bills must be supported by receipts.] *

7. The expenses procedure will be monitored by ......*(insert name).* Any abuse by employees will result in disciplinary action and, depending on the circumstances, is likely to be treated as gross misconduct resulting in summary dismissal (e.g. where an employee has intentionally sought to defraud the Company).

delete as appropriate

Homeworkers' expenses policy

The increasing tendency for individuals to work from home raises the question of which home-related costs can be reimbursed tax free by an employer. So you'll need a company policy making it clear to your employees which expenses come with a tax bill.

WORKING FROM HOME

There has been a very large increase in the number of employees who work from home. A question often asked by employers is how the additional expenses the employee will incur as a result of working from home are to be met and what the correct tax treatment is for reimbursed expenses and the provision of equipment. The basic position is that if you provide an employee with equipment that can be used privately, there will be a benefits charge. It would be very difficult for you to keep a check on the use of the equipment and HMRC should accept that the private use is insignificant as long as you have a clearly stated **Homeworkers' Expenses Policy** setting out when private use is accepted. In this case, there will be no tax or Class 1A NI due. The additional costs of such things as heating and lighting which arise due to working at home can be reimbursed without any charge to tax and NI.

HOMEWORKERS' EXPENSES POLICY

Provision of equipment

The Company will supply you with the necessary equipment that may reasonably be required to enable the contract to be performed from home. This may include some of the following:

- telephone
- fax machine
- laptop/desktop computer
- computer software/licences
- printer
- photocopier
- desk and chair
- filing cabinet(s)
- desk stationery
- writing materials.

An inventory will be kept as a means of recording the equipment supplied and you will be required to sign for the receipt of any equipment provided.

The equipment shall at all times remain the property of the Company, not be used for private purposes and be returned by you when you cease working from home. All equipment supplied by the Company will be covered under the Company's insurance policy.

Travel

You will be recorded as having your home as your permanent place of work. Therefore travel between your home and the Company's premises, or any other location visited on behalf of the Company, is regarded as business travel and will be reimbursed under the normal expenses policy rules.

Telephone

See the separate provision of home telephone policy.

Additional home expenses

The additional costs of such things as heating and lighting, which arise due to you working from home will be reimbursed at a flat rate of [£4 per week] [£18 per month].

Incidental overnight expenses policy

If an employee has to stay away overnight on business, there are some tax and NI-free expense payments you can make. To achieve this you'll need to have a company policy in place to avoid an employee claming for the wrong amounts, which is what a visiting tax inspector would go looking for.

EXPENSE PAYMENTS

If an employee has to stay away overnight on business, then you can pay them up to £5 per night in the UK (£10 per night overseas) tax and NI free, in respect of their miscellaneous personal expenses such as telephone calls home or newspapers. If you want to do this, you need to have procedures in place to make sure you don't accidentally reimburse the expenses twice - first as part of the hotel bill and second via the employee's separate expense claim. This can be achieved by following the **Incidental Overnight Expenses Policy**.

INCIDENTAL OVERNIGHT EXPENSES POLICY

Personal incidental expenses, for example, personal telephone calls, newspapers, laundry etc., incurred whilst staying away overnight on Company business, must be excluded from the accommodation costs. They should be identified separately on the invoice by the hotel, or if this is not possible, highlighted by the claimant and excluded on the expenses claim. The Company will not reimburse invoices that do not show any personal expense items separately. The employee will be responsible for these costs.

The maximum amount that can be claimed per night on personal incidental expenses is equivalent to HMRC's tax-free limits which are currently:

Staying away in the United Kingdom	£5.00 (inclusive of VAT)
Staying away overseas	£10.00 (inclusive of VAT)

The employee must reimburse the Company for any amounts in excess of these tax-free limits by 6 July, following the tax year in which the overpayment occurred.

Loan agreement

To avoid a payment to an employee/director being treated (and taxed) as additional salary, you could reclassify it as a fixed-rate loan. What documentation will HMRC need to be convinced about this?

INEXPENSIVE FINANCE

The income tax paid by a director or employee on a subsidised loan provided by their employer is based on the difference between the interest rate actually charged and what is known as the "official rate". At present the official rate is 3.25%, subject to review in the event of significant changes. So a loan from your company remains a source of inexpensive, relatively short-term finance.

As evidence that the payments made to the employees should be treated as (NI free) loans rather than (NIable) salary, it's important to keep a copy of the **Loan Agreement**, setting out the terms of the loan and any interest that the employee has to pay.

LOAN AGREEMENT

THIS AGREEMENT is made on ....*(insert date)*

BETWEEN

(1) ....*(insert name of Lender)* of .... *(insert address of Lender)* ("the Lender"); and

(2) ....*(insert name of Borrower)* of ....*(insert address of Borrower)* (the "Borrower").

1. Amount of Loan

The Lender will lend to the Borrower and the Borrower will borrow from the Lender the sum of £....*(insert amount)* "the Loan" on the terms which follow.

2. Interest

The Borrower shall pay to the Lender interest on the Loan at the rate of ....*(insert figure)* per annum quarterly on the last day of each of the months of [March June September and December] [January April July and October] [February May August and November] in each year. The first such payment to be made on whichever of the interest payment dates first occurs after the advance of the Loan and to be in respect of the period from and including the date of such advance until the next interest payment date.

3. Repayment

Unless otherwise agreed, the Borrower may only repay the Loan by a single payment on .... *(insert date).*

4. Compulsory repayment subject to demand

The Lender may, by notice in writing to the Borrower, demand the immediate payment of all moneys due or incurred by the Borrower to the Lender together with all interest and any other sums forthwith (or otherwise as the Lender may require) at any time if the Borrower does not pay on the due date any money which may have become due hereunder or under any document supplemental hereto.

Loan record

A taxable benefit may arise where a director or employee is provided with a loan, either interest free or at a favourable rate of interest. Use this document to calculate what, if anything, you need to declare to HMRC.

IMPORTANT TO MONITOR

Where a low-interest or interest-free loan is made to a P11D employee or director, a benefit-in-kind will have to be included if it's more than £10,000 (£5,000 for 2013/14 and earlier) at any time during the year. You can use HMRC's P11D working sheet to calculate the amount you need to include. However, it's important to monitor loans to ensure that they don't go over the limit, so complete a **Loan Record** for all loans taken out by employees and directors.

Note. It is the combined outstanding value of all loans made to the director/employee throughout the year that must be less than £10,000 if a report to HMRC is to be avoided.

LOAN RECORD

Record the date, description and amount the loan increases (+) or decreases (-) by.

For example:

Company name:				Employee's/Director's name:		
Subject: *Record of transactions going through the loan account*						
Date of transaction	**Description of the transaction**	**Your initials**	**Loan increases ("+") £0.00**	**Loan decreases ("-") £0.00**	**Balance outstanding £0.00**	
1 January 2014	Opening balance	PJ	-	-	2,000.00	
17 January 2014	Interest charged	PJ	100		2,100.00	
28 January 2014	Amount repaid	PJ		(200)	1,900.00	
2 February 2014	Further advance	PJ	500		2,400.00	

Mobile phone declaration

The old rule was that you could have as many mobile phones as you liked, tax and NI free. Now it's down to one per employee. If you have more than one, you will need to declare which one is to be your tax-exempt phone.

CHOOSE YOUR EXEMPT PHONE

The tax exemption for employees who are provided with a mobile phone changed on 6 April 2006. Directors/employees provided with more than one new phone by their company will need to consider which is to be the "exempt" phone and which the "taxable" phone. They can record this choice with a **Mobile Phone Declaration**. It will probably be for the phone they make most of their personal calls from. If the other phone is used strictly for business calls, then although in theory it's taxable, there is no tax bill because there are no private calls.

MOBILE PHONE DECLARATION

To: ....*(insert name of Company)*

I hereby elect that my new company mobile phone (number ..………….......... *(insert mobile phone number)*) shall be treated as my "exempt from tax" phone.

Signed ....

Date ....

Note.   This declaration is only necessary if you have more than one mobile phone issued to you.

Overpayment of expenses policy

Annual reporting by employers of benefits in kind to HMRC (on P11Ds) also doubles up as a requirement to report expenses payments to employees. The trap is that these are taxable unless the employee can claim a deduction for them. So accidental reimbursement of non-business expenses comes with a tax bill. How can you avoid this?

CLAIM THE EXPENSES BACK

Have a clear **Overpayment of Expenses Policy** so that you are entitled to claim any overpayment of expenses back from the employee before the next P11D is prepared.

These overpayments can be taken straight from the employee's salary. With round sum allowances, keep a record of who has them and how much they are for, what they are meant to cover and why they haven't been put through the payroll.

OVERPAYMENT OF EXPENSES POLICY

The Company reserves the right to make deductions from salary where there has been, for whatever reason, an overpayment of expenses. Overpayments will be recovered in accordance with the principles outlined below which apply to all staff employed by the Company.

Principles

1. Overpayments remain Company money at all times. They never form part of employees' salary or remuneration packages.

2. Overpayments will be recoverable direct from the employee's salary or wage.

3. It is the employee's duty to notify the Company if they believe an overpayment has been made.

4. Where the Company discovers an overpayment, the employee will be notified in writing, giving precise details of the overpayment.

5. Where an employee is leaving the Company, the overpayment must be repaid in full upon termination of employment. In these circumstances, the sum will be deducted from final pay due at termination, without prior agreement.

6. Where an overpayment is discovered following issue of final pay, the Company reserves the right to pursue recovery of any outstanding amounts through the courts.

P11D dispensation letter

Where HMRC has granted you a dispensation that allows you to exclude details of certain benefits and expenses paid to your company's directors and employees, you must inform them of this.

LET THEM KNOW

You can apply to HMRC for a PAYE dispensation which, if approved, means that certain benefits and expenses you pay or provide to your employees don't need to be declared on Form P11D. This is a useful time saving arrangement, but you must notify those affected.

Where your employees are required to complete a personal self-assessment tax return they must declare all benefits and expense payments they receive in connection with their job. However, they should not do this for items that are covered by a dispensation. Use our **P11D Dispensation Letter** to tell them about this.

P11D DISPENSATION LETTER

…………………………………………. *(insert employee name)*

………………………………………… *(insert employee address)*

……………………………………………

……………………………………………

……………………………………………

……………………………………………

………………………………………… *(insert date)*

Dear ……….. *(insert employee's name)*

Form P11D for *(insert year, e.g. 2014/15)*

The Company is required to provide you with information it has reported to HMRC on Form P11D in respect of benefits and expense payments paid or provided to you for the tax year ended April 5 ………. *(insert year).*

HMRC granted the company a dispensation on ………………….. *(insert date)* that released it from the requirement to report the benefits and expense payments of the types shown at the bottom of this letter.

I am writing to tell you that because of the dispensation we [are not required to complete a form P11D for you] [have completed a P11D which excludes the types of benefit or expense listed below] (*delete as appropriate*). *(If you are required to complete a tax return you should not include details of any benefits or expenses payments paid by the Company to you where they are covered by the dispensation.)*

Yours sincerely

…………………………………………. *(insert name)*

…………………………………………. *(insert position)*

Benefits and expenses covered by dispensation:

For example travel and subsistence payments

PAYE settlement agreement letter

The point of a PAYE settlement agreement with HMRC is that you (the employer) formally agree to meet the tax liability in respect of certain employee benefits/expenses. When would you actually need such an agreement?

TO MAINTAIN GOODWILL

Where you make a minor or irregular gift to an employee that gives rise to a tax or NI liability, you can use a PAYE settlement agreement (PSA) to pay any liability on behalf of the employee. The use of a PSA involves grossing up the payment for tax and NI so the value received by the employee represents the net value after deductions. This does make giving a free gift more expensive, but it will help to maintain staff goodwill - a gift isn't always so welcome if it comes with a large tax bill. HMRC doesn't provide a standard application form, so to set up a PSA you need to write to your local inspector using the **PAYE Settlement Agreement Letter**, describing which gifts you want to include. If the item is subject to tax or NI at the time of making the gift, the agreement must be in place before the payment is made. In other cases, they can be agreed after the event. The tax due must be paid by 19 October following the year to which the PSA relates. A PSA has to be renewed on an annual basis but this is usually a formality.

PAYE SETTLEMENT AGREEMENT LETTER

HMRC

....*(insert address)*

....

....

....

....*(insert date)*

Your ref ....*(insert your employer's PAYE tax reference)*

Dear Sirs

Year-ended 5 April ....*(insert year)*

We request a PAYE settlement agreement for the ..... *(insert year)* tax year onwards. We wish the agreement to cover liabilities arising on the following items:

....*(insert details)*

....*(insert details)*

....*(insert details)*

The liabilities arising will be calculated on a grossed-up basis and by reference to the number of basic rate and higher rate taxpayers covered by the agreement.

The tax and Class 1B NI liability arising will be paid to HMRC by 19 October, following the end of each tax year.

We should be grateful if you would confirm your acceptance or otherwise of this before 6 July ......*(insert year)* in order that we may file form P11D in a timely manner.

Yours faithfully

....*(insert name)*

Provision of home telephone policy

If you have an employee who works from home, you might think it's a good idea to have a landline installed there. What will HMRC expect to find about this in your paperwork?

A CLEAR BUSINESS NEED

Where you pay directly for a telephone in your employee's home, they will have to pay tax and you'll have to pay employers' NI on the cost of the line rental and calls, less any amount reimbursed by the employee. However, if:

- you (the employer) are the subscriber

- there's a clear business need for the telephone

- you have procedures in place to ensure that private calls are kept to a minimum or that the employee reimburses you for the full cost of their private calls, then the employee won't be taxed on the line rental or the calls and you'll save the employers' NI.

Use our **Provision of Home Telephone Policy** to document your procedures.

PROVISION OF HOME TELEPHONE POLICY

If you are required to work from home on a regular basis, the Company will provide you with a separate telephone line for business use only.

The Company will contract directly with the telephone services provider.

You will reimburse the Company for the cost of any private calls made on a monthly basis at the actual cost (inclusive of VAT) as shown on the telephone services invoice.

Agreement

I agree to reimburse the Company for the actual cost of any private calls made using the separate business telephone line provided to me.

Signed ....

Dated ....

Scale rate clearance letter

Where you have a number of directors or employees who travel frequently, you can easily reduce the work involved in processing their expense claims by giving them a round sum allowance to cover items such as lunch and dinner. However, to avoid having to deduct tax on the amounts paid, you'll need to agree these scale rate payments with HMRC.

ROUND SUM ALLOWANCE

If you provide directors and employees with a round sum allowance for some common business expenses like hotels and meals, these are known as scale rate payments.

As long as the directors and employees are actually spending the round sum payments on business expenses, you can ask HMRC to agree the scale rates by sending a **Scale Rate Clearance Letter.** By doing this, you won't need to deduct tax from the payments under PAYE.

HMRC should agree as long as it is satisfied that the calculation of your scale rate is based on genuine expenses incurred in the past and there is no profit element in it for the employee. You will need evidence (e.g. receipts) that supports the scale rate that you want to use. As it may be impractical for you to obtain evidence of expenditure for every employee, HMRC will accept a random sample of at least 10% of your employees for a period of one month (see HMRC's Employment Income Manual EIM05210).

BENCHMARK RATES

Alternatively, to avoid carrying out the time-consuming sampling exercise, you could use HMRC's benchmark scale rates which are:

Breakfast rate (irregular early starters only) - up to £5, where the employee leaves home earlier than usual and before 6.00am and incurs a cost for breakfast taken away from home. However, if the employee regularly leaves home before 6.00am because of, for example, working an early shift, they can't claim the allowance tax free.

One meal rate (five-hour rate) - up to £5, where the employee has been away from home or the normal place of work for a period of at least five hours and has incurred the cost of a meal.

Two meal rate (ten-hour rate) - up to £10, where the employee has been away from home or the normal place of work for a period of at least ten hours and has incurred the cost of a meal or meals.

Late evening meal rate (irregular late finishers only) - up to £15, where the employee has to work later than usual, finishes work after 8.00pm having worked the normal day and has to buy a meal which would usually have been taken at home. If an allowance under the five or ten-hour rule is paid, the late meal allowance may also be paid.

These are national rates, so if they're not enough, you're still entitled to demonstrate the need to pay more by undertaking a sampling exercise.

SCALE RATE CLEARANCE LETTER

HMRC

.... *(insert address)*

....

....

....

.... *(insert date)*

Dear Sirs

.... ***(insert employer's PAYE reference)***

We intend to start making the following round sum payments to employees with regard to travelling and subsistence expenses:

Accommodation:

London	Per night, exclusive of meals	£75
	Per night, inclusive of meals	£96
Elsewhere	Per night, exclusive of meals	£60
	Per night, inclusive of meals	£85

Meals (when staying away overnight):		
	Breakfast	£6
	Midday meal	£7
	Evening meal	£15

We do not consider that there is any profit element in the above rates. The rates are based on a random sample of 10% of employees' expenses for the month of ....*(insert month and year)* and are reasonable in relation to the employment involved.

Under company policy, the employee will still need to fill out an expenses claim form before a payment is made.

We should be grateful if you would confirm that we can make these round sum payments without the need for them to be taxed under PAYE.

Yours faithfully

.... *(insert signature)*

Travel expenses policy

To a get a reporting dispensation for specific expenses (e.g. travel) from HMRC you'll need company polices which you can prove have been effectively communicated to your employees.

BUSINESS TRAVEL

Including a **Travel Expenses Policy** in your staff handbook will provide evidence to HMRC that you only reimburse qualifying travel expenses. This will make it more likely to grant a dispensation for these expenses, reducing the amount of work you need to do at the tax year-end.

Our policy makes reference to home-to-office travel, which should not be included in business travel claims plus the type of transport which should be used on business trips. It specifies that public transport as opposed to taxis should be used wherever possible. (Own car use is covered in a separate policy.)

TRAVEL EXPENSES POLICY

Business journeys
You can claim the full cost of any travel expenses incurred while you are on Company business.

Home-to-office travel
You are responsible for the cost of travel between your home and normal place of work. Costs relating to such journeys should not be included in claims for business travel expenses. When a business journey starts or ends at home, the amount claimed should be arrived at by deducting the normal mileage travelled to and/or from home and the office.

Travel by taxi
Use of public transport (bus, tube or train etc.) is encouraged and should be used wherever possible, for business purposes. However, it is recognised that the use of a taxi may, in the following circumstances, be the most effective mode of transport:
• where equipment or heavy baggage is being carried
• when no public transport is available, especially when travelling early in the morning or late at night
• when the claimant is pregnant or has a temporary or permanent disability
• where personal or financial security is an issue
• when it is important to save time
• when in an unfamiliar area and uncertain about public transport.

You should obtain an official receipt from the taxi driver to substantiate your subsequent travel expense claim, and you must state clearly on the expense form the reason for use of a taxi.

Travel by train
You are encouraged to take advantage of special deals where possible, and will be expected to travel in standard class. Expense forms must have attached to them as supporting documentation either the actual train tickets or a receipt from the train company. If a receipt is required, this should be requested at the time of ticket purchase as they may not be issued automatically.

Travel using own car
See separate policy.

Trivial benefits letter

There is no lower limit beneath which benefits are not taxed. However, you can apply to HMRC for agreement to allow you to exclude certain small gifts to staff from your reporting on the grounds that they're trivial.

SMALL GIFTS

HMRC allows you to give small gifts to staff tax and NI free. The gift has to be "trivial" and cannot be money, something capable of being exchanged for money, or a voucher. The examples given in HMRC's manual **(EIM21863 - Employment Income Manual and NIM16690 - National Insurance Manual)** are items such as a turkey, a bottle of wine or a box of chocolates. The gift cannot be in reward for services as an employee. So a reward for the year's hard work will still attract tax and NI whereas a seasonal goodwill gift will not. The total cost may be substantial where a large number of staff is involved, but provided the individual value of the gift remains trivial, no liability should arise - the number of employees has no bearing. As there's currently no clear definition of trivial (HMRC is considering introducing a statutory exemption for trivial benefits), use the **Trivial Benefits Letter** to seek confirmation and agreement from HMRC that the gifts concerned can be left off the P11Ds.

TRIVIAL BENEFITS LETTER

HMRC

.... *(insert address)*

....

....

....

.... *(insert date)*

Dear Sirs

.... ***(insert employer's PAYE reference)***

We intend to provide the following benefits to employees which we regard to be minor and trivial in nature *(insert description of benefit, number of staff to whom it is provided, unit cost and total cost to employer).*

We should be grateful if you would confirm that these benefits would be regarded as trivial in nature and also confirm in writing that tax and NI will not be sought and that details of the benefit need not be reported on the P11D/P9D.

(The following paragraph to be used in the event that benefits are covered by a PSA.)

We have provided the following benefits to employees and which are covered by a PAYE settlement agreement dated .... *(insert date of PSA).*

.... *(insert description of benefit, number of staff to whom it is provided, unit cost and total cost to employer).*

We should be grateful if you could confirm that these benefits will be regarded as trivial and confirm in writing that tax and NI will not be sought. Please amend the PAYE settlement accordingly and confirm the amendment in writing.

Yours faithfully

.... *(insert signature)*

Using your own car on company business policy

If employees use their own vehicles for business journeys, you should have a company policy which spells out the situation regarding insurance, parking and mileage rates at which you will reimburse them.

TAX-FREE MILEAGE

Include the **Using Your Own Car on Company Business Policy** if employees use their own vehicles for business journeys. You will need to make it clear that it's the employee's responsibility to ensure they have adequate insurance in place and that the company will not be liable for any parking fines issued. Provided the reimbursement made to them is not more than HMRC's approved tax-free mileage rates, no benefit in kind will need to be reported on the P11D and it does not need to be included in a dispensation. However, HMRC will expect you to keep a record of the amounts paid and the business journeys they are for.

USING YOUR OWN CAR ON COMPANY BUSINESS POLICY

Insurance

As the driver is personally liable for any incident, you should ensure that your own private motor vehicle policy is comprehensive and permits the use of your own vehicle for the purposes of business use. The cost of acquiring this is reflected in the mileage rate.

Mileage rates

The Company will reimburse you for business mileage at the following rates:

First 10,000 miles in a tax year - 45p per mile
Over 10,000 miles - 25p per mile

Mileage claims should be made at the end of each month by completing the mileage record form and expenses claim form.

Parking fines

Parking fines and other penalties will not be reimbursed by the company.

Congestion charge and tolls

Congestion charges and tolls incurred during business trips will be reimbursed. However, any congestion charges and tolls incurred as part of your home-to-work journey will not be reimbursed. Penalties for non-payment will not be paid or reimbursed by the company.

Section 6

Employee remuneration

Childcare voucher policy

Where childcare is provided by way of voucher, the first £55* per week is tax-free if certain conditions are met. Whether you administer a voucher scheme yourself or engage an external voucher provider, you need a policy in place to demonstrate that your scheme meets the requirements.

AN APPROVED SCHEME

To meet the HMRC's conditions for tax-free childcare, you will need evidence that the scheme is offered to all employees, so include a **Childcare Voucher Policy** in your staff handbook.

Our policy sets out two major conditions of the scheme. Firstly, that the child must be: **(1)** the employee's child or stepchild; or **(2)** living with the employee and the employee has parental responsibility for them. Secondly, that the voucher must be used to pay for qualifying childcare by a registered childcare provider. Be aware that certain exclusions exist to prevent particular types of care from qualifying. Relief will be denied if the care is provided by a relative of the child, wholly or mainly in the child's home. A relative is a parent, grandparent, aunt, uncle, brother or sister *"whether by blood, half blood or civil partnership"*.

Childcare provided by relatives can be qualifying if **all** the following apply:

- the relative is a registered or approved childcare provider
- the care is provided away from the child's home
- the care is provided to non-related children in addition to the related child.

* £28 per week if earnings are above the higher rate tax threshold, and £25 (£22 from 6 April 2011 to 5 April 2013) per week if earnings are above the additional rate tax threshold.

CHILDCARE VOUCHER POLICY

The Company operates a childcare voucher scheme which is open to all employees. The scheme is implemented as a salary sacrifice arrangement where you exchange part of your salary for childcare vouchers.

The first £55 per week (£28 if higher rate tax applies to earnings or £25 per week if additional rate applies) of the voucher's face value will be given to you tax and NI-free as long as the following conditions are met:

Condition A:
- the child must be your actual child or stepchild and be maintained (wholly or partly) at your expense or
- the child must be living with you and you have parental responsibility for the child.

Condition B:
Childcare vouchers can only be used to pay for any form of qualifying childcare. Qualifying childcare includes:
- registered childminders, nurseries and play schemes
- school or council-run out of hours clubs
- extended school scheme run by school governing bodies
- childcare schemes run by approved providers
- childcare given in the child's home by an appropriate registered agency worker
- approved foster carers (but not for their own foster children).

Childcare provided by a relative of the child wholly or mainly in the child's home does not qualify even where the childminder is registered.

Condition C:
The child is a qualifying child. The child will qualify until 1 September following their 15th birthday (or 16th birthday if the child is disabled).

Procedure
You will provide details of your childcare provider to the Company including their registration or approval number together with the date the relevant registration expires.

You must notify the Company of any changes in registration or approval status of your child's carer or changes in childcare arrangements.

The Company will provide you with a childcare voucher. You will then give this voucher to your qualifying childcare provider. The childcare provider will then sign the voucher and send it to the Company for reimbursement. There is no cost to the childcare provider in receiving payment through childcare vouchers.

Golden hello payment letter

An inducement payment will sometimes be made to a new employee. Such a payment will normally be taxable. Exceptionally, it may be tax-free if you can demonstrate that the payment is not by reason of the employment. How can you establish this?

LUMP SUM PAYMENT

A "golden hello" is a popular term for a lump sum payment received on the taking up of employment. Normally, tax is due on these payments as if they were salary. However, if the payment is an inducement rather than a reward for future services, then it could be tax free if it satisfies the following conditions:

- it must be clear from the facts that the payment is an inducement and not a reward for future services

- if possible, the payment should be made before the employment commences (particularly for NI purposes this means before acceptance of employment is put in writing by letter or otherwise)

- the payment must not be returnable if the person does not take up the employment

- from case law, it is more likely that the payment will be accepted as tax free if the prospective employee has previously been self-employed and is giving up some right or asset to take up the employment.

Make sure the payment is accompanied by the **Golden Hello Payment Letter** which indicates that the payment is an inducement.

GOLDEN HELLO PAYMENT LETTER

....*(insert prospective employee's name and address)*
....
....
....

....*(insert date)*

Dear ....*(insert name)*

Please find enclosed a payment of ....*(enter amount)* as compensation for giving up ....*(enter details of right or asset given up)* on the assumption that you will decide to join our company. This is a one-off non-returnable payment and in no way represents reward for future services. No tax has been deducted from this inducement payment as it falls outside the provisions of s.225 **Income Tax (Earnings and Pensions) Act 2003**.

Yours sincerely

....*(insert signature)*

Enc

PAYE audit checklist

If you receive a letter telling you that HMRC wants to carry out a review of your payroll records, use our checklist as an aide memoire to the best way to handle the visiting inspector?

PREPARE FOR A VISIT

HMRC has a legal right to inspect your payroll records to confirm that you are paying the correct amount of tax and NI. It sees these visits as a chance to make some easy money. Most PAYE inspections result in some mistakes being found and HMRC will often calculate the "lost" tax and NI over a period of four years plus the current year. This period may even be extended if it suspects that tax has been withheld on purpose. It may also seek penalties, although these will normally depend on the size of the error and how much the employer co-operates. Use the **PAYE Audit Checklist** to help prepare for an impending visit.

PAYE AUDIT CHECKLIST

Before the visit

1. Contact HMRC to arrange a specific time for the visit (if you can't make the suggested dates, offer an alternative within one month of the original).

2. Check that the following records are complete for at least the last twelve months:

- PAYE/RTI

- (if applicable) copies of CIS payment summaries to contractors (together with the subcontractors' supporting invoices)

- hours worked, such as clock cards or timesheets

- cash book

- petty cash analysis

- company policies relating to expenses and benefits

- employment and subcontractor contracts

- dividend vouchers and board minutes for dividends voted to director/employee shareholders

- directors' loan account schedules.

3. Print off hard copies of your payroll records, e.g. the P11s or equivalent (you don't want HMRC to have access to your computer files).

4. Review a sample of the records yourself. If you find any problem areas, seek advice from your accountant.

5. Arrange for a separate office to be available so that your visitors' movements are controlled.

6. Send a memo to all staff saying that the HMRC auditors are only doing their job and they are not trying to catch them out. Remember to leave a copy of this in the visitors' room.

During the visit

1. Collect all the records requested and place them in the visitors' room.

2. Ask to see the official's ID card on arrival and make a note of their name.

3. Give them your extension number so that all the queries and requests come straight to you.

4. Make sure your diary is clear for the day so that you can be available as and when required.

5. If photocopies are requested, get your own staff to do it. Get them to keep a record of what's to be copied.

6. Disclose voluntarily, at an early stage, any known irregularities to demonstrate a willingness to co-operate.

7. Don't give an off-the-cuff answer if you're not sure of your facts. Don't speculate - if you don't know, say so.

8. Make notes during the visit of any answers given by you or your staff to ensure later correspondence can be checked against the facts stated during the visit.

9. Don't sign any statements during the visit - take time to check them thoroughly and have them vetted by an advisor, adding in anything necessary to clarify confusing points.

Payment in lieu of notice clause

You might decide that an individual should not work out their notice period and that they should be paid for this period instead. You need to take account of the legal more than the tax issues when drafting documentation for dealing with a termination payment. So where should you start?

TO USE A **PILON** CLAUSE?

In the absence of an express **Pay in Lieu of Notice** (PILON) **Clause**, pay in lieu of notice will be regarded as a payment of compensation in connection with termination of employment, i.e. damages for breach of contract. With a PILON clause, pay in lieu of notice is regarded as wages payable under the contract of employment. So why does it matter what it's classed as? Firstly, with a PILON clause, you can limit the amount payable, as our pay in lieu of notice clause does, to basic salary only. Where you have to pay damages for breach of contract, the damages must put the employee in the position they would have been had the contract been properly performed. This means you will have to compensate the employee for the loss of any benefits in kind during what would have been the notice period. Secondly, since without a PILON clause you are technically committing a breach of contract if you pay in lieu, there is a high risk that an employment tribunal will hold that you cannot then enforce the other provisions of the contract. If the contract contained restrictive covenants, this could cause you a major headache if you can't rely on them. Thirdly, the employee could try and bring a claim for wrongful dismissal against you if you have paid in lieu with no PILON clause, although if you have adequately compensated them for their loss, their claim may have little substance. And finally, the clause does not say you have to pay in lieu of notice - it only says that you may do so, so the choice is yours. You can still require the employee to work out their notice period even with a PILON clause.

PAY IN LIEU OF NOTICE CLAUSE

The Company reserves the right to make a payment in lieu of notice for all or any part of your notice period on the termination of your employment. This provision, which is at the Company's absolute discretion, applies whether notice to terminate the contract is given by you or by the Company and your contract can be terminated summarily at any time with immediate effect under the terms of this clause by notification of the termination of the contract being given to you in exercise of this clause.

Any such payment will consist solely of basic salary (as at the date of termination) and shall be subject to such deductions of income tax and National Insurance contributions as the Company is required or authorised to make.

For the avoidance of doubt, the payment in lieu of notice shall not include any element relating to:

    a) any bonus or commission payments that might otherwise have been due during the period for which the payment in lieu is made
    b) any payment in respect of benefits which you would have been entitled to receive during the period for which the payment in lieu is made; and
    c) any payment in respect of any annual leave entitlement that would have accrued during the period for which the payment in lieu is made.

[The Company may pay any sums due under this clause in equal monthly instalments until the date end of the period for which the payment in lieu is made.]

You have no right to receive a payment in lieu of notice unless the Company exercises its discretion under this clause.

In addition, the payment in lieu of notice will not be payable, or can be recovered in full by the Company, if, following the termination of your employment, the Company subsequently discovers that you had committed an act of gross misconduct during your employment which would have entitled it to terminate your contract of employment without notice or payment in lieu of notice.

Personal appreciation gift letter

There are very few circumstances in which an employee can receive tax-free cash from an employer. But a gift made "on personal grounds" or as a "mark of appreciation" might be one of them. How do you go about proving this to the HMRC's satisfaction?

A PERSONAL GIFT

Where cash paid to an employee is a genuine gift in recognition of some personal quality, and is in no sense a reward for performing duties past, present or future, then it can be paid tax-free. HMRC's instructions **(EIM01460 - Employment Income Manual)** suggest that to escape liability, possible reasons for the gift might be: "on personal grounds, e.g. a wedding present, or as a mark of personal esteem or appreciation". Always keep a copy of the covering letter with any such payment to provide evidence, if required, to HMRC. Our **Personal Appreciation Gift Letter** will serve this purpose.

PERSONAL APPRECIATION GIFT LETTER

....*(insert date)*

Dear ....*(insert employee name)*

We would like to make a cash gift to you of .... *(insert amount).* This gift is in recognition of ....*(insert reasons for payment)* and is not in any way related to your employment duties. In accordance with HMRC's instructions, it is treated as a tax-free payment.

If you need to complete a tax return, this payment should be entered in the additional information box to disclose it, but you should refer to it as a "gift on personal grounds" or "mark of personal esteem or appreciation", whichever is appropriate. Also state that you therefore consider the gift as "not taxable".

Yours sincerely

....*(insert signature)*

Register of child carers

HMRC imposes quite an onerous record-keeping burden on employers when it comes to childcare. In particular, for the tax-free relief to apply the care must be "qualifying childcare", defined as registered or approved care. Therefore, you need to check this and keep a record of the results.

STRINGENT RECORD KEEPING

The HMRC Employer Helpbook E18 - "How to help your employees with childcare" indicates that you will need to keep the following:

(1) A copy of your scheme rules that includes a requirement for employees to notify you of any change in circumstances in relation to the child or childcare.

(2) A record of the childcare provider's name and registration or approval number.

(3) A note of when the childcare provider's approval is going to expire.

According to guidance in E18, the following can provide information on whether a particular carer is registered or approved: in England phone the Ofsted helpline 0300 123 1231 or go to http://www.ofsted.gov.uk; in Scotland http://www.scswis.com/; in Northern Ireland, http://www.nidirect.gov.uk/childcare; and in Wales http:/www.wales.gov.uk.

To comply with the age restriction requirements (a person is considered a child until after 1 September following their 15th birthday or 16th birthday if disabled), you also need to keep a record of the date of birth of an employee's youngest child.

Use our **Register of Child Carers** to keep detailed records of all the carers involved with your childcare voucher scheme.

REGISTER OF CHILD CARERS

Employee name	NI number	Date of birth of youngest child	Name of childcare provider	Address 1	Address 2	Address 3	Postcode	Telephone number	Registration number	Date of expiry of registration

Salary sacrifice letter

If you currently pay all of your employees' salaries as cash, then real savings can be made if they sacrifice part of it for a non-taxable benefit such as pension contributions, childcare vouchers or even additional holiday.

BENEFIT IN KIND

Remuneration can take the form of cash, which will always be fully taxable if it is for duties performed in the past, present or future, or as a benefit in-kind, which may or may not be taxable. The ideal situation is to provide a benefit that is tax deductible for the employer, and generates neither an income tax charge for the employee nor an NI charge for either of you. It is essential that you get your employees to sign a **Salary Sacrifice Letter** before the reduced salary is due to take effect, otherwise HMRC will insist that they are taxed on the benefit as if it were pay.

SALARY SACRIFICE LETTER

....*(insert name)*

....*(insert address)*

Date . ...*(insert date)*

Dear ....*(insert name)*

Consent in Relation to Deductions from Salary

Please note that with effect from .... *(insert date)* your basic salary will be reduced by ...... *(insert amount)* from ....*(insert amount)* to ....*(insert amount)*. The sum of .... *(insert amount)* is to be:

[paid into the Company's pension scheme for your benefit upon retirement*]

[paid as childcare vouchers*]

[paid as .... *(insert details of benefit)*]

[In addition, you have elected to take ....*(insert amount)* additional holidays and, therefore, your basic salary will be reduced by a further .... *(insert amount)* (i.e.1/260th of gross salary per additional holiday day taken) to .... *(insert amount).*]

Your notional salary (which will form the basis of any future salary reviews) will be your gross salary at your last salary review.

These new agreed terms represent a permanent variation to your contract of employment. The Staff Handbook sets out the rules for the scheme and you must read it carefully before signing the attached copy of this letter and returning it to .... *(insert name)* to signify your agreement to the changes and deductions detailed above.

Yours sincerely

I have read the scheme rules as set out in the Staff Handbook and agree to the changes and deductions outlined above and acknowledge that these new agreed terms represent a permanent variation to my contract of employment.

* delete as appropriate

....*(insert signature)*

....*(insert date)*

Salary sacrifice policy

If you want to implement a salary sacrifice scheme in your company, make sure you insert the relevant policy in your staff handbook. Your policy will need specific details regarding extra holiday or pension provision.

SCHEME PARTICULARS

Including a **Salary Sacrifice Policy** in your staff handbook is important both to convey the details of the scheme and to point out any drawbacks. For example, a sacrifice requires a permanent alteration to the employment contract and could have an effect on borrowing capacity for mortgages and credit cards as well as possibly interfering with benefits and work-related payments such as statutory maternity, adoption, paternity or sick pay.

SALARY SACRIFICE POLICY

The Company offers a salary sacrifice scheme, whereby it can [pay your pension contribution directly into your pension scheme] and/or [you can "buy" additional holiday*] and/or [provide you with childcare vouchers*] in exchange for a salary sacrifice. This saves both the Company and you from paying NI contributions (and in some instances, tax) upon the salary that you sacrifice.

Details are as follows: .... *(insert salary sacrifice policy - holidays and/or pensions and/or other details).*

Scheme rules

Each participant in the scheme will be notified of a notional salary that will form the basis of any future salary reviews.

The Company reserves the right to withdraw the salary sacrifice scheme at the end of the Company's financial year which runs from ..……….…… *(insert start date)* to ...……………. *(insert end date).*

Gross salaries will be adjusted from the date of joining the salary sacrifice scheme onwards.

A sacrifice must not cause the rate of pay to be less than the prevailing minimum wage figure.

Drawbacks of salary sacrifice

As the sacrifice is a permanent alteration to the contract of employment, you will not have the right to revert to the original (higher) salary level; otherwise the sacrifice will not be valid in the eyes of the HMRC and if they deem the sacrifice to be ineffective for any reason, then the contribution will be treated as a benefit-in-kind and could therefore increase tax and NI liabilities rather than reducing them.

However, in exceptional circumstances, if you are forced to revert to the original (higher) salary level, this can only be done via a mutually agreed variance of your contract in writing and cannot be subsequently rescinded. Such action may affect the taxation consequences of the original salary sacrifice as explained above. Applications must be made in writing to ...………........ *(insert name).*

It must be remembered that, as the name of the salary sacrifice scheme suggests, salary must be genuinely sacrificed, therefore any other benefits or transactions which are based on salary or the amount of NI contributions made will be affected. For example:

Any borrowing levels, such as mortgage, credit card limits, personal loans etc., which are set in conjunction with the salary level, will be affected by the sacrifice.

Contribution-based state benefits such as Employment and Support Allowance, Job Seekers' Allowance and State Pension will be affected by any salary sacrifice, as will earnings related benefits such as maternity allowance and, where the revised salary falls between the lower earnings limit (LEL) and the upper earnings limited (UEL), the State Second Pension.

Work related payments such as statutory maternity, adoption, paternity or sick pay will also be adversely affected by a sacrifice. If the sacrifice reduces the salary to less than the LEL then entitlement to Basic State Pension would be affected.

Working tax credit and child tax credit could also be affected by any sacrifice.

* delete as appropriate

Sample childcare voucher

You can sacrifice part of your salary for childcare vouchers to save on tax and NI. For a fee, you can use a childcare voucher company to administer the scheme for you, but there's nothing to stop you printing your own vouchers and issuing them to employees.

TAX-FREE VOUCHERS

The first £55* per week of childcare vouchers that you give to an employee is both tax and NI free for those who joined the scheme before April 2011. By offering employees the opportunity to take a pay cut in exchange for childcare vouchers, you will save the 13.8% employers' NI and the employee will save both tax and NI. Use our **Sample Childcare Voucher** as a template for your own vouchers. The employee can use the vouchers to pay for approved childcare, e.g. a registered childminder. They give the voucher to the approved child carer who then sends it back to you for the company to settle.

Note. The £55* limit is per parent not per child so if both parents work in the same company, they can receive up to £110 a week tax free (via separate vouchers).

*For those users who joined the scheme from April 2011, the weekly tax and NI free amount has been reduced to £28 and £25 (£22 from 6 April 2011 to 5 April 2013) per week for higher and additional rate taxpayers respectively.

SAMPLE CHILDCARE VOUCHER

Front of voucher:

Childcare Voucher	Childcare Voucher		
			Valid only in the UK
Childcare			
(Insert employee's name)		Value:	£ *(insert amount)*
(Insert employee's number)	*(insert employee's name)*		
(Insert employer's contact address)		Valid until:	*(insert date)* (valid for twelve months)
	(insert your company name and address)		Childcarer's signature
Value: £*(insert amount)*			Childcarer's name *(please print)*
	Employee's signature		
			Childcarer's registration number
Voucher No:	Voucher No:		

Reverse of voucher:

Conditions of Acceptance

Voucher validity:

1. Valid until the last day of the month printed on the front of this voucher

2. This voucher may only be used by a legally entitled person/childcare organisation

For further information contact the personnel department on *(insert telephone number)*

Notice to childcare provider:

The employee must sign the front of the voucher and the childcare provider must counter sign the voucher before it will be paid.

Completed forms should be returned to
(insert your company name and address)

In the UK this voucher remains the property of

(insert your company name) and is not transferable

(insert company address)

Issued by:

Address:

Settlement agreement

When you want to prevent an employee from issuing proceedings in relation to the infringement of their statutory employment rights on termination of their employment, consider going down the settlement agreement route. This is an alternative to going through time-consuming dismissal procedures. In addition, it can also be used to settle serious employee disputes, such as allegations of constructive dismissal or unlawful discrimination.

NEGOTIATED TERMINATIONS

Sometimes, it will become necessary to dismiss an employee in circumstances where you want to prevent them from issuing employment tribunal or other court proceedings against you in relation to infringement of their statutory (or contractual) employment rights. This may happen in relation to senior employees when there is an existing employment dispute but you do not propose to go through formal dismissal procedures because you want them out as soon as possible. In such circumstances, you should hold a "without prejudice" meeting to discuss the termination package in return for their signing a **Settlement Agreement**. This is essentially a formal, legally binding agreement made between an employer and employee (or ex-employee) in which the employee agrees not to pursue particular claims they believe they have in relation to their employment or its termination, in return for a financial settlement from the employer.

LEGAL FORMALITIES

In order for a settlement agreement to be legally binding, a number of important statutory conditions must be fulfilled as follows: - the agreement must be in writing - it must relate to the "particular proceedings" - the employee must have received independent legal advice from a relevant adviser as to the terms and effect of the agreement and, in particular, its effect on their ability to pursue their rights before an employment tribunal - there must be in force, when the adviser gives the legal advice, a contract of insurance or professional indemnity insurance covering the risk of a claim by the employee in respect of loss arising as a result of the advice - the agreement must identify the relevant adviser - the agreement must state that the conditions regulating settlement agreements under the relevant Act(s) are satisfied.

The people who are eligible as "relevant advisers" are: - qualified lawyers (solicitors holding a practising certificate or barristers in practice or employed to give legal advice) - officers, officials, employees or members of an independent trade union, provided that they have been certified in writing by the union as competent and authorised to give advice - employees or volunteer workers at advice centres giving free legal advice, provided that they have been certified in writing by the advice centre as competent and authorised to give advice - fellows of the Institute of Legal Executives employed by solicitors' practices.

WITHOUT PREJUDICE

The "without prejudice" meeting should only take place with the employee's consent and they should be warned in advance that you wish to have a meeting of this nature. There should also be a pre-existing employment dispute with the employee and the discussion must be a genuine attempt to settle the dispute. As stated above, the employee is required by law to seek independent legal advice as to the terms and effects of a settlement agreement. You should ensure that all correspondence in connection with the negotiation of the agreement is marked "without prejudice" (including the draft agreement itself) so as to avoid disclosure of it should negotiations for settlement break down prior to signature of the agreement. Marking correspondence this way will prevent the use of it in any subsequent legal proceedings. Bear in mind that if settlement negotiations do break down, you're likely to be left with a disgruntled employee!

SECTION 111A OF THE EMPLOYMENT RIGHTS ACT 1996

S.111A provides that any offer made or discussions held by an employer with a view to terminating an employee's employment on agreed terms is inadmissible as evidence in any subsequent ordinary unfair dismissal claim - and in this case there doesn't need to be a pre-existing employment dispute between the parties as there does for the "without prejudice" principle to apply.

Unfortunately, there are three exceptions to this rule. Firstly, it doesn't apply where the employee claims to have been dismissed for an automatically unfair reason. Secondly, if there was "improper behaviour" by the employer, the employment tribunal may then determine the extent to which it's just to admit the evidence. Thirdly, the employer may reserve the right to refer to the settlement offer for the purposes of any tribunal determination on costs/expenses. In addition, it doesn't prevent the evidence being admitted in other types of claims, such as those for discrimination or breach of contract. Few employers are likely to be in a position to discount the possibility of an automatic unfair dismissal, discrimination or other claim when conducting a settlement discussion with an employee and therefore, in practice, conducting "open" pre-termination discussions under s.111A, as an alternative to going through a lengthy dismissal procedure, is not without significant risk.

However, if you do decide to do this, you can still use our settlement agreement but it will not be on a "without prejudice" basis and, if settlement negotiations break down, you will only be able to prevent evidence of the meeting and any correspondence being admissible in any ordinary unfair dismissal proceedings where there has been no improper behaviour on your part.

THE EMPLOYEE'S PARTICULAR COMPLAINTS

A settlement agreement may be used to settle one or more employee complaints. In drafting it, you should make clear each of the specific complaints being settled and refer to the relevant statutory provisions because, as identified above, the settlement agreement must relate to the "particular proceedings". Particulars of the complaints made by the employee and of the particular allegations made in them must be inserted into the settlement agreement in the form of a brief factual and legal description. A 'blanket agreement' simply signing away all of an employee's employment rights, or one which lists every form of employment right known to the law, will probably not be a valid settlement agreement. It's always better to get legal advice on drafting a settlement agreement because it is a complex legal document which has to be tailored to fit the circumstances of the particular case. Our settlement agreement is a good starting point for you but you will need to consider the clauses in detail to decide which are relevant. In addition, not all sums payable under a settlement agreement are tax-free so speak to your accountant if you're unsure.

SETTLEMENT AGREEMENT

([WITHOUT PREJUDICE AND] SUBJECT TO CONTRACT)

THIS AGREEMENT is made on ....*(insert date)*

AND IS MADE BETWEEN:

.... Limited *(insert name of Company)* whose registered office is at .... *(insert registered office details)* ("the Company"); and

.... *(insert name of employee)* of .... *(insert address of employee)* ("the Employee")

RECITALS:

1. The Employee has been employed by the Company under the terms of a contract of employment dated ....*(insert date)*.

2. This Agreement satisfies the conditions regulating settlement agreements under:

   • Section 203 of the Employment Rights Act 1996

   • Section 147 of the Equality Act 2010

   • Regulation 9 of the Part-Time Workers (Prevention of Less Favourable Treatment Regulations 2000

   • Regulation 10 of the Fixed-Term Employees (Prevention of Less Favourable Treatment Regulations 2002

   • Regulation 35 of the Working Time Regulations 1998

   • Section 49 of the National Minimum Wage Act 1998

   • Section 288 of the Trade Union and Labour Relations (Consolidation) Act 1992

   • Regulation 40 of the Information and Consultation of Employees Regulations 2004

   • Regulation 18 of the Transfer of Undertakings (Protection of Employment) Regulations 2006.

3. The Company enters into this Agreement without any admission of liability.

THE COMPANY AND THE EMPLOYEE AGREE AS FOLLOWS:

1. The employment of the Employee by the Company (will terminate/terminated) on .... *(insert date)* ("the Termination Date"). The Employee will continue to be bound by their contract of employment until the Termination Date.

2. This Agreement is in full and final settlement of all employment related claims that the Employee has and/or may have against the Company arising out of their employment or the termination of employment whether or not they are or could be in the contemplation of the parties at the time of signing this Agreement.

3. The Employee has notified the Company that they consider they are in a position to make a complaint of .... *(insert details of employee's complaint, for example unfair dismissal, sex discrimination, race discrimination, etc. and refer to any correspondence in which the employee has notified the Company of their complaint).*

4. The Company shall:

4.1. Provided the Employee continues to comply with their contract of employment, pay the Employee their salary up to and including the Termination Date and pay in lieu of any accrued but unused annual leave entitlement. These sums will be subject to normal statutory income tax and National Insurance deductions.

4.2. Without admission of any liability as claimed or otherwise, pay to the Employee by way of compensation for termination of employment the sum of £ ....*(insert amount)* [within 14 days of the signing of this Agreement] [in .... *(insert number)* equal monthly instalments on the .... *(insert details)* day of every month commencing on .... *(insert date)* and ending on .... *(insert date)*] ("the Payment"). Of this sum, £ .... *(insert amount)* will be paid free of income tax and National Insurance deductions pursuant to section 401 of the Income Tax (Earnings and Pensions) Act 2003 and the balance of £ .... *(insert amount)* will be paid after the deduction of income tax and National Insurance.

4.3. Pay the Employee a sum in respect of .... *(insert number)* (weeks/months) pay in lieu of (contractual/statutory minimum) notice within 14 days of the signing of this Agreement ("the Pay in Lieu"). This sum will be (subject to normal statutory income tax and National Insurance deductions/paid free of income tax and National Insurance deductions as it does not represent contractual remuneration).*

4.4. Pay the Employee a statutory redundancy payment of £ ....*(insert amount)*, paid free of income tax and National Insurance deductions, within 14 days of the signing of this Agreement.*

4.5. Provide the Employee with a P45 within 14 days of the signing of this Agreement.

4.6. Continue, up to and including ....*(insert date)*, to provide the Employee with the benefits of (*life assurance, private medical insurance and pension scheme contributions) on the same terms as those benefits were provided to the Employee as at the Termination Date.*

4.7. Permit the Employee to retain their company car until .... *(insert date)* on the same terms and conditions as they enjoyed the use of that car during their employment but on the understanding that no mileage incurred by the Employee will constitute travel between their home and the Company's premises nor will it constitute business travel.*

4.8. Provide the Employee with a reference in the attached terms should the same be requested by any potential employer of the Employee.*

4.9. Contribute to the Employee's legal costs in seeking advice as to the terms and effects of this Agreement up to a maximum of £ .... *(insert amount)* plus VAT on receipt of an appropriate invoice in the Employee's name and marked payable by the Company and which refers to the advice.*

4.10. Arrange for the Employee to be provided with outplacement counselling up to a maximum cost to the Company of £ .... *(insert amount)* plus VAT with .... *(insert name of outplacement company)* subject to receipt of a valid invoice from .... *(insert name of outplacement company)* and provided that the outplacement counselling must start before .... *(insert date)* and must be completed by no later than .... *(insert date).**

(*Delete as appropriate.)

5. The Employee shall:

5.1. Not divulge to any third party at any time any trade secrets or other confidential information belonging to the Company or any of its associated companies and not use such secrets or information for their own benefit or that of any third party.

5.2. Return to the Company all correspondence, documents, equipment, computer hardware and software, keys, cards and any other property which belongs to the Company or relates in any way to the business of the Company or any associated company which are in their possession or under their control and shall at the same time confirm to the Company that no copies have been retained (whether held in electronic or hard copy form).

5.3. Refrain from disclosing the contents of the terms of this Agreement other than to their spouse, partner, lawyer or accountant except as may be ordered by any court, government agency or as required by law.

5.4. Refrain from making or publishing any statements, whether oral or written, touching upon or concerning their relationship with the Company or any associated company or relating to the circumstances surrounding the termination of their employment which are critical, adverse, negative or derogatory, or which might be detrimental to the interests of the Company or any associated company or its or their clients, customers, officers or employees or which might reasonably be considered to insult, damage or impugn its or their reputation. For the avoidance of doubt, this includes statements or comments made on social media or business networking websites. Social media and business networking websites are public forums even if account privacy settings are set at a restricted level.

5.5. Accept full responsibility for the payment of any income tax and National Insurance deductions not already made by the Company and indemnify and keep indemnified the Company against all and any liabilities to income tax or National Insurance deductions, interest, penalties and costs which the Company may incur in respect of or by reason of the Payment or the Pay in Lieu and, within seven days of being informed by the Company of the amount of any such tax or National Insurance assessment, pay to the Company an equivalent amount.

5.6. Warrant as a strict condition of this Agreement that they have not at the date of this Agreement accepted, either verbally or in writing, an offer of employment or entered into a contract for services or a consultancy agreement with any person, firm or company.

5.7. Warrant as a strict condition of this Agreement that they have not knowingly committed any breach of duty to the Company, or any breach of the terms of their contract of employment, and that there are no circumstances of which they are aware or ought reasonably to be aware which would constitute a repudiatory or material breach on the Employee's part of any express or implied term of their contract of employment which would entitle or have entitled the Company to terminate their contract of employment without notice or payment in lieu of notice.

[5.8. Resign from their directorship (and as Company Secretary) with the Company with effect from the Termination Date, execute a letter of resignation in such form as the Company shall require and execute any further documents as may be necessary to give full effect to the resignation, including completing any formalities necessary to secure the amendment of records at Companies House.]

5.9. [Forthwith withdraw their employment tribunal claim number .... *(insert number)* and] not present to an employment tribunal or any other court any claim under clause 5.10 which has been settled by the terms of this Agreement.

5.10. Accept the payments and actions of the Company set out above in full and final settlement of all or any claims arising out of their contract of employment or its termination which they may have against the Company or any associated company or any of its or their officers or employees, whether such claims are known or unknown to the Employee and whether or not they are or could be in the Employee's contemplation at the time of signing this Agreement or which may arise in the future, and whether such claims are contractual, statutory or otherwise, including, but not limited to, claims for:

    5.10.1   Damages for breach of contract (whether brought before any employment tribunal or otherwise) in respect of any salary, holiday pay, notice pay, bonus or commission due.*

    5.10.2   Unauthorised deduction from wages or right to an itemised pay statement under the Employment Rights Act 1996.*

    5.10.3   Holiday pay under the Working Time Regulations 1998 or any other breach of the Working Time Regulations 1998.*

    5.10.4   Breach of the National Minimum Wage Act 1998.*

    5.10.5   Unfair dismissal, including constructive dismissal, under the Employment Rights Act 1996.*

    5.10.6   Detriment under the Employment Rights Act 1996.*

    5.10.7   A written statement of particulars of employment or reasons for dismissal under the Employment Rights Act 1996.*

    5.10.8   Damages arising out of the Company's failure to deal with the Employee's grievance in accordance with the ACAS Code of Practice on Disciplinary and Grievance Procedures or the Company's grievance procedure, including breach of the statutory right to be accompanied.*

    5.10.9   Damages arising out of the Company's failure to deal with disciplinary action against and/or dismissal of the Employee in accordance with the ACAS Code of Practice on Disciplinary and Grievance Procedures or the Company's disciplinary procedure, including breach of the statutory right to be accompanied.*

5.10.10 Detriment relating to the making of a protected disclosure under the Public Interest Disclosure Act 1998.*

5.10.11 Contractual or statutory redundancy pay.*

5.10.12 Discrimination by reason of age, disability, gender reassignment, marriage and civil partnership, pregnancy and maternity, race, religion or belief, sex or sexual orientation under the Equality Act 2010 or other discrimination legislation.*

5.10.13 Victimisation in connection with age, disability, gender reassignment, marriage and civil partnership, pregnancy and maternity, race, religion or belief, sex or sexual orientation under the Equality Act 2010 or other discrimination legislation.*

5.10.14 Harassment in connection with age, disability, gender reassignment, race, religion or belief, sex or sexual orientation under the Equality Act 2010 or other discrimination legislation.*

5.10.15 A failure to make reasonable adjustments in connection with disability under the Equality Act 2010 or other discrimination legislation.*

5.10.16 Equality of terms or equal pay under the Equality Act 2010 or other equality legislation.*

5.10.17 Discrimination, victimisation or detriment related to trade union membership or activity.*

5.10.18 Less favourable treatment on account of being a part-time worker or arising out of the Part-time Workers (Prevention of Less Favourable Treatment) Regulations 2000.*

5.10.19 Less favourable treatment on account of being a fixed-term employee or arising out of the Fixed-term Employees (Prevention of Less Favourable Treatment) Regulations 2002.*

5.10.20 Any claim arising out of the transfer of an undertaking under the Transfer of Undertakings (Protection of Employment) Regulations 2006.*

5.10.21 A guarantee payment under the Employment Rights Act 1996.*

5.10.22 A failure to collectively consult on redundancy under the Trade Union and Labour Relations (Consolidation) Act 1992 or any other claim under the Trade Union and Labour Relations (Consolidation) Act 1992.*

5.10.23 Distress, anxiety or financial loss caused by harassment under the Protection from Harassment Act 1997.*

5.10.24 Personal injury arising out of or relating to any acts of discrimination, harassment, victimisation or detriment.*

5.10.25 Any other claim arising under UK statute, UK common law or under EU law (except any accrued and future pension rights).

5.10.26 .... *(insert details of any other claims raised by the Employee).*

(*Delete as appropriate.)

5.11. Accept that if their rights under any of the provisions referred to above have not been validly and lawfully excluded by the provisions of this Agreement and if they should purport to exercise such rights (or any of them) and if an employment tribunal or other court should find that any compensation is payable to the Employee by the Company as a consequence, the monies paid to the Employee under this Agreement shall be deducted (so far as may be requisite) from any award of compensation in diminution or extinction thereof.

5.12. Accept that the Payment and the Pay in Lieu to be made by the Company pursuant to the terms of clauses 4.2 and 4.3 of this Agreement are entirely conditional on the Employee's compliance with the warranties given in clauses 5.6 and 5.7 of this Agreement.

5.13. Agree that if they materially breach any material provision of this Agreement, they will repay to the Company a sum equivalent to the Payment and/or the Pay in Lieu (after deduction of all income tax and National Insurance contributions which may be due) and that the Payment and/or the Payment in Lieu is recoverable from them by the Company as a debt.

5.14. In consideration of the Payment and the Pay in Lieu made pursuant to the terms of clauses 4.2 and 4.3, after the Termination Date upon request provide the Company with all reasonable assistance in potential or ongoing litigation, proceedings, investigations or enquiries concerning its business in relation to any matter which the Employee directly or indirectly dealt with in the course of their employment.

[5.15.Take reasonable steps to find alternative work during the instalment period set out for the Payment in clause 4.2 and notify the Company of any income received in this period. In any month in which the Employee receives income from paid work that is less than the instalment due, the instalment will be reduced by the amount of that income. If the Employee's income from paid work in any month is the same or more than the instalment due for that month, the instalments will cease and the Employee's right to receive any further instalments will cease from the date upon which the work producing such income commenced.]

[5.16.Continue to be bound by the terms and conditions in their contract of employment which relate to restrictive covenants: see clause .... *(insert number).*]

6.   This Agreement sets out the entire settlement between the parties and supersedes all prior discussions between them or their advisers and all statements, representations, terms and conditions, warranties, guarantees, proposals, communications and understandings whenever given and whether orally or in writing.

7.   If any term of this Agreement is held to be illegal, invalid or unenforceable, in whole or in part, such part shall be deemed not to form part of the Agreement but the legality, validity or enforceability of the remainder of the Agreement shall not be affected.

8.   This Agreement shall be governed by and construed in accordance with the law of [England and Wales] [Scotland] and the parties agree to submit to the exclusive jurisdiction of the courts in [England and Wales] [Scotland] in relation to any matter connected with this Agreement.

9.   Notwithstanding that this Agreement is marked "subject to contract", once it has been signed and dated by all parties it will become an open and binding document (subject to clause 5.3).

10. The solicitor .... *(insert name of solicitor)* of .... *(insert firm name)* of .... *(insert firm address)* confirms that they have provided the Employee with independent legal advice as to the terms and effect of this Agreement and, in particular, its effect upon their ability to pursue their rights before an employment tribunal or other court. By signing this Agreement, the solicitor who provided the advice warrants that they hold a current practising certificate and that the firm currently maintains the level of indemnity cover required of it by the Solicitors Regulation Authority covering the risk of a claim by the

Employee in respect of any loss arising in consequence of the advice they have received.

SIGNED:

.... Director
For and on behalf of the Company

SIGNED:

.... *(insert name of employee)*

SIGNED:

.... *(insert name of solicitor)*
For and on behalf of .... *(insert name of firm)*

Staff suggestion scheme rules

You might want to reward your employees for certain ideas that contribute to the success of your business. Previously by concession, this is now a statutory exemption. However, there are conditions you'll have to meet.

FINANCIALLY BENEFICIAL

A little-known way of giving employees tax and NI free cash is through a staff suggestion scheme. The scheme needs to be formally set up, but that doesn't take much doing. You tell the staff that they will receive a small payment in return for ideas that may help the business. A really good idea that is taken up by the company will get a larger reward. Write down the amounts you plan to pay, and how you would like the ideas to be put forward. Pin these **Staff Suggestion Scheme Rules** to the office notice board so everyone can see them, and you are all set to start the suggestion scheme.

You can pay up to £25 for any suggestion but if it is implemented and likely to financially benefit the company, you can pay out the lower of: £5,000; and 50% of the expected financial benefit in the first year (or 10% of the expected financial benefit over five years if greater).

STAFF SUGGESTION SCHEME RULES

1. The scheme is open to all employees on equal terms.

2. An award may be made, at the discretion of the board of directors (or by a committee appointed by the board), for a suggestion which is outside the scope of the employee's normal duties. In this regard, the test is whether or not the employee, taking account of his experience, could have been expected to put forward such a suggestion as part of his normal duties.

3. An encouragement award may be made in respect of a suggestion which, although it will not be implemented, has some intrinsic merit and/or reflects meritorious effort on the part of the employee in making the suggestion. The amount of such an award will not exceed £25.

4. Alternatively, an implementation award may be made directly to the employee(s) concerned, following a decision to implement the suggestion. The amount of any such award will be based on the degree of improvement in efficiency and/or effectiveness likely to be achieved, measured by reference to:

   • the prospective financial benefits and the period over which they are expected to accrue, and

   • the importance of the subject matter having regard to the nature of the Company's business

   and will not exceed the greater of:

   • 50% of the expected net financial benefit during the first year of implementation, or

   • 10% of the expected net financial benefit over a period of up to five years

   subject to an overall limit of £5,000.

5. Where a suggestion is put forward by more than one employee, any implementation award arising from it will be divided between them on a reasonable basis.

6. The scheme does not apply to any sums paid to an employee in respect of the exploitation or disposal of rights in an invention devised by them (such as patent rights, know-how, etc.)

7. The company does not guarantee to any employee that an award will be tax free. However, any encouragement award under this scheme is likely to be non-taxable, as is the first £5,000 of any implementation award (divided as necessary between two or more employees where 5. above applies).

8. The decision of the board on the amount of any award, and on the terms of the scheme generally, shall be final.

Suggestion scheme ideas log

In certain circumstances tax rules permit employers to reward staff tax free for ideas. But HMRC will want to see some evidence of the benefit the business has derived from this payment. Is there a simple way of doing this?

Log the ideas

The really clever bit of a staff suggestion scheme is that even if you get snowed under with suggestions, you get to pick the ideas to be used or rewarded so you decide who gets the money. HMRC, however, will want to know all about the tax-free amounts you are giving to your staff, so you need to estimate and record the cost savings or extra sales revenue for any suggestion that you use. Use the **Suggestion Scheme Ideas Log** for this.

SUGGESTION SCHEME IDEAS LOG

Employee name	NI number	Suggestion	Implemented (Y/N)	Estimated financial benefit to company	Amount paid* £

* The maximum you can pay tax-free for suggestions that are not implemented is £25. The maximum you can pay tax free for implemented suggestions is the lower of £5,000 and 50% of the expected financial benefit in the first year (or 10% of the expected financial benefit over five years).

Termination payment letter

You need to take account of both the legal and tax issues when drafting documentation for dealing with a termination payment. But if you don't have any employment issues with the departing employee it's arguable that the payment can be made tax free (subject to the £30,000 tax-free limit). Use this document to improve your chances of HMRC agreeing with you.

THE TAX-FREE LETTER

The major downside to having a **Pay in Lieu of Notice** (PILON) **Clause**, is that the payment is then taxable as it's a payment of earnings made under the contract of employment. Without a PILON clause, it's arguable that the payment is tax free (subject to the £30,000 tax-free limit) as compensation for loss of employment. If you don't have any employment issues with the departing employee you should enclose a **Termination Payment Letter** with the payment to the employee. This should explain that you have not made a payment in lieu of notice but have breached the employee's contract. It is therefore seen as damages for the breach. Further evidence that a termination payment is tax free.

TERMINATION PAYMENT LETTER

....(*insert name*)

....(*insert address*)

Date ....(*insert date*)

Dear ....(*insert name of employee*)

WITHOUT PREJUDICE

In accordance with the compromise agreement dated ..... (*insert date*), we enclose a cheque in the sum of .... (*insert amount*). This ex gratia payment solely relates to compensation for termination of your employment and was not provided for in your employment contract. Of this sum, £......(*insert amount up to £30,000*) has been made without deduction of income tax or NI. [The balance of £ ..... (*insert amount over £30,000, if applicable*) has been paid with income tax and NI deducted as follows:

Gross payment	£...................................(*insert amount*)	
Income tax	£...................................(*insert amount*)	
NI	£...................................(*insert amount*)	
Payment enclosed	£...................................(*insert amount*)]	

Yours sincerely

....(*insert signature and name of author*)

Enc

Termination payment minutes

You can use company law formalities to support your case that a termination payment is not ordinary earnings and hence not taxable (up to a £30,000 limit). What's involved?

Ex GRATIA MINUTES

If possible, agreement to make a termination payment, and its approval by the board using **Termination Payment Minutes**, should be made after employment ceases. Where this is not practicable, any reference in any minute or document should be as brief as possible and refer to the payment only as being "ex gratia". Don't refer to it as "consideration for past services" as this will almost certainly make it taxable.

TERMINATION PAYMENT MINUTES

....*(insert company name)* LIMITED

MINUTES OF A DIRECTORS' MEETING

HELD ON ....*(insert date)*

IT WAS RESOLVED that following the termination of ....'s *(insert employee's name)* employment with the Company, a payment of £......*(insert amount)* should be made to them as compensation for breach of contract.

....*(insert signature)*

Chairperson

Section 7

IHT

Chattel lease

In order for a gift to be effective for inheritance tax purposes, you must be excluded from "benefiting", other than to a limited extent, from the asset once you've given it away. But if you were to lease it back in some way, what terms should be included in the lease agreement to ensure it isn't treated as a gift with reservation of benefit?

Not a gift with reservation

If you officially pass some valuable antiques on to the next generation but keep these objects in your own home, they would still be subject to inheritance tax (IHT) treatment. And, similarly, all the time that such a benefit exists, the value of a property remains subject to IHT on your death. So you can't give away a property and still have possession of it. Or can you?

The payment of a market rent/fee normally avoids this so-called gift with reservation problem for IHT. Ideally, this figure should be established by agreement, see our **Chattel Lease**, between two professional valuers acting for the two sides. To ratify the agreement the rent/fee must, of course, actually be paid during the tax year.

CHATTEL LEASE

THIS AGREEMENT is made on ....*(insert date)*

BETWEEN

(1) ....*(insert name of Parents')* ("the Parents"); and

(2) ....*(insert name of Children)* (the "Children").

THE BACKGROUND

The Children are the beneficial owners of the chattels set out in the Schedule below (the "Chattels")

The Children wish to allow the Parents the use and enjoyment of the Chattels on the basis of full consideration payable by the Parents.

THE AGREEMENT

1. Bailment

The Children grant a lease of the Chattels to the Parents for the following term and generally on the terms and conditions following:

2. The term

The term of the lease shall be equal to the joint lives and life of the survivor of the Parents, terminable either:

2.1   Upon six months' written notice given by either party

2.2   Immediately upon default of any obligations contained in Clause 9

2.3   Immediately upon both the Parents or the survivor of them becoming mentally incapable within the meaning of s. 94 (2) of the **Mental Health Act 2007,** as amended.

3. Ownership

3.1   The Children retain the ownership of the Chattels

3.2   The Children reserve the right to fix any plating or other means of identification to the Chattels

3.3   The Parents covenant not (nor take steps) to sell, deal, charge or part with the Chattels in any other way contrary to the ownership of the Children

3.4   The Parents will immediately pay any sum required to remove any lien which may arise over the Chattels.

4. Enjoyment and housing

4.1 The Children covenant with the Parents (provided the Parents pay the rent and perform the Parents' covenants) that the parents shall peaceably hold and enjoy the Chattels during the term without any interruption by the Children or any person rightfully claiming under or in trust of any of them

4.2 The Chattels shall be housed at ....*(insert name of property)* or at other locations from time to time agreed between the Parents and the Children.

5. Rental

5.1 The initial annual rental for the Chattels shall be £....*(insert figure)* per annum (which is agreed by the Children and the Parents to reflect the current open market rental value of the Chattels)

5.2 The rental shall be paid annually; the first year's rental is due on the signing of this agreement (and the Children acknowledge receipt of it); further annual rental payments shall be due on the anniversaries of this agreement.

5.3 The rental shall be reviewable by agreement at three yearly intervals from the date of this Agreement to ensure that the Parents give full consideration for the use and enjoyment of the Chattels. In default of agreement, the reviewed rent shall be determined by a valuer appointed by the President for the time being of the National Association of Valuers and Auctioneers (NAVA) acting as expert and not an arbitrator, either party shall be at liberty to request the President to make such an appointment.

6. Insurance

6.1 The Parents will insure the Chattels for their full replacement cost comprehensively against all risk with the interest of the Children noted on the Policy and will duly and punctually pay all premiums and on request will promptly produce the insurance policy and proof of payment of premiums to the Children. All claims under such insurance policy will be dealt with in accordance with the written direction of the Children. All claims and moneys received by the Parents under such insurance policy shall be held by the Parents in trust for the Children.

7. Preservation and repair

7.1 The Parents undertake to preserve the Chattels

7.2 The Parents undertake to keep the Chattels clean and in good and substantial repair and will bear the cost of any repairs not covered by insurance

7.3 The Parents will permit the Children and any person authorised by them at any reasonable hour to view or survey the state and condition of the Chattels

7.4 The Parents will forthwith after being required to do so by the Children make good any want of repair in the Chattels.

PROVIDED that nothing in this clause shall require the Parents to maintain the Chattels in anything other than their current condition or require the Parents to improve or put the Chattels into first rate condition.

8. Security

8.1 The Parents undertake to put in place, maintain and bear the cost of such security arrangements as are from time to time agreed between the Parents and Children or as are reasonably stipulated by the Children to reflect the requirements of any relevant insurance company, advice from the Police or advice otherwise specifically received from a specialist security company engaged for the purpose.

9. Default

If the Parents default in the punctual payment of any of the instalments of rent provided for, or default in the payment of the insurance premiums as provided for, or default in the performance of any of the terms and conditions of this agreement, the Children may immediately retake possession of the Chattels, without notice to the Parents, with or without legal process, and the parents by this agreement authorise and empower the Children to enter the premises or other places where the Chattels may be found to take and carry away the Chattels. All moneys due under this agreement shall become immediately due and payable plus all reasonable costs of repossession.

EXECUTED ON .... *(insert date)*

.... *(insert signatures "the Parents")*

.... *(insert signatures "the Children")*

Deed of gift

Sometimes it's necessary to transfer a share of your property to someone else in order to make your estate planning arrangements more effective. What simple documentation can you use to effect this?

SHARE YOUR ESTATE

A **Deed of Gift** document can be used, for example, to transfer assets from one spouse to another, *"I gift half of [....] to my spouse in order to formally recognise that they have contributed to the home in other than monetary terms."* Where no money changes hands, a deed of gift is an economical way of effecting the transfer.

Indeed, if the home is currently in one name only, then whoever owns it should make a gift of half of it to the other spouse.

If you are using a deed of gift you will also need a tenancy-in-common declaration to show how the property is now split.

DEED OF GIFT

THIS DEED OF GIFT is made the ..... *(insert day)* day of ..... *(insert month)* 20[ ]

BETWEEN

....*(insert name)* called the [Donor][Assignor] on the one part and

.... *(insert name)* called the [Donee][Assignee] of the other part

WHEREAS

1. The donor is the beneficial owner of the ..... *(insert description of asset)* called the [Asset] [the policy] [particulars] [of which are contained in the schedule hereto].

2. The donor wishes to transfer the Asset and the full benefit thereof to the donee by way of gift.

NOW THIS DEED WITNESSES as follows

1. In consideration of his/her [natural] love and affection for the Donee, the Donor as beneficial owner HEREBY [GIFTS][ASSIGNS] the [Asset] for the full benefit thereof and all moneys thereby to become payable under or by virtue thereof to the [Donee][Assignee] by way of gift TO HOLD the same absolutely.

[2. The Assignor covenants with the Assignee that the policy is now valid and in full force.

3. The Assignor shall not be under any obligation whatever to keep up the policy or to reinstate it the same if it shall become void, nor shall the Assignee have any right whatever by way of lien or otherwise reimbursement of any sum or sums paid or provided by the assignor to keep up or reinstate the policy.

4. It is hereby certified that this instrument falls within category L in the Schedule to the **Stamp Duty (Exempt Instruments) Regulations 1987**.]

IN WITNESS whereof the parties hereto have signed this instrument as their deed in the presence of the persons mentioned below the day and year first above written.

[THE SCHEDULE ABOVE REFERED TO IS:

Life office: .... *(insert life office)*

Policy number(s): .... *(insert policy number)*

Life/lives assured: .... *(insert life/lives assured)*]

Signed and delivered by the said [Donor][Assignor]..

In the presence of:
Witness: ....*(insert name)*

Address: ....*(insert address)*

Occupation: ....*(insert occupation)*

Signed and delivered by the said [Donee][Assignee] ....

In the presence of:
Witness: ....*(insert name)*

Address: ....*(insert address)*

Occupation: ....*(insert occupation)*

Deed of variation

It's nice to be remembered in a will but this can leave you with an inheritance tax problem of your own. However, you can vary the terms of the original will so that the bequest passes directly to someone else instead.

NEXT GENERATION

A gift (known as a disposition) made by a deceased person may be disclaimed or varied, e.g. passed on to the next generation, within two years from the date of death. You can use our **Deed of Variation**, to be signed in the presence of a witness, to achieve this. The deed needs to be signed by all the beneficiaries of the will affected by the change.

DEED OF VARIATION

THIS DEED OF VARIATION dated ....*(insert date)* is made between:

1. "the Executors" .... *(insert names)* .... *(insert addresses)*

2. "the original Beneficiary" .... *(insert name)*

3. "the substituted Beneficiary" .... *(insert name)* .... *(insert address)*

WHEREAS

1.1 XY ("the Deceased") died on ..... *(insert date)* having made his/her Will ("the Will") on ..... *(insert date)* and probate of the Will was granted to the Executors by the District Probate Registry on ..... *(insert date).*

1.2 AB ("the original Beneficiary") was entitled to ..... from the deceased's estate.

2. The original Beneficiary and the substituted Beneficiary:

2.1 agree that the provisions of the Schedule shall be construed as if they constituted the deceased's will and his/her estate shall be administered accordingly.

2.2 direct the Executors to distribute the estate of the deceased in accordance with the provisions of the Schedule.

3. The parties elect for section 142(1) of the **Inheritance Tax Act 1984** and section 62(6) of the **Taxation of Chargeable Gains Act 1992** to apply to this deed.

4. It is certified that this instrument falls within category M in the schedule to the **Stamp Duty (Exempt Instruments) Regulations 1987**.

SCHEDULE

Signed as a Deed by the Executors……………………………………………………………

in the presence of .... *(insert name)*

.... *(insert address)*

Signed as a Deed by the Original Beneficiary……………………………………………………

in the presence of .... *(insert name)*

.... *(insert address)*

....*(insert occupation)*

Signed as a Deed by the substituted Beneficiary…………………………………………………..

in the presence of .... *(insert name)*

.... *(insert address)*
.... *(insert occupation)*

Inheritance tax fall in value claim

Where, within four years of the date of the deceased's death, a property in their estate is sold at open market value for less than probate value, you can make a claim to recalculate the inheritance tax using the sale value instead.

CONDITIONS

A number of conditions must be satisfied:

- a claim must be made within seven years of the date of death

- all sales within the first three years following of death must be taken into account, whether they were for more or less than probate value; sales made in the fourth year for more than the date of death value can be ignored.

- a claim must be made by the "appropriate person". This is the person liable to pay the Inheritance Tax on the land or buildings. Usually this will be the executor of the estate, but might be the trustees of a trust created by a will or in some cases the beneficiary. **Note.** The relief is not available where the property has already been transferred to a beneficiary and later sold.

OTHER SITUATIONS

Although HMRC may try to object, there's nothing specific in the legislation to disallow a claim to be made, even where the property was sold for more than the probate value. This would reduce the combined Inheritance Tax and capital gains tax bill on the property where the rate of the former is lower than the latter. One situation in which this applies is where the property in question is subject to 50% business property relief. The effective rate of IHT is this instance is 20% while CGT might be payable at up to 28%.

Use our **Inheritance Tax Fall in Value Claim** to save time and ensure you include all the information HMRC needs to process your claim. Alternatively, you can use HMRC's Form IHT38 (http://www. hmrc.gov.uk/cto/forms/iht38.pdf).

INHERITANCE TAX FALL IN VALUE CLAIM

HM Revenue & Customs
Trusts & Estates
Inheritance Tax
Ferrers House
PO Box 38
Castle Meadow Road
NOTTINGHAM
NG2 1BB

………………… *(insert date)*

Dear Sir

………………… *(insert the name of the deceased and Inheritance Tax reference if known)*

Claim for fall in value relief in respect of land or buildings - s.191 IHTA 1984

The land and buildings listed in the attached schedule, which were included in the estate of the above named, were sold for a different value than that recorded for probate purposes. Therefore, please accept this letter as a claim to substitute the probate value with the sale price.

[We understand that this claim is provisional until three years have passed since the deceased's death.] *

Yours faithfully

……………………….
(insert name)

……………………..
(insert capacity in which you are making the claim, e.g. executor)

Delete where either three years have elapsed or there was only one area of land or building included in the estate.

Schedule

Details of all sales of land and buildings within three years of the date are listed in the table below. Sales of buildings in the fourth year are also shown where these were at a value less than that reported for probate.

Address of land or buildings	Date of sale	Probate value	Sale value before the deduction of costs

Letter of wishes

A discretionary will allows your executors to make decisions according to current tax law, the final assets in the estate and the financial/health circumstances of the beneficiaries. However, there is a way you can specify how you would prefer your estate to be distributed.

IHT PLANNING

In your will you will have appointed executors to manage your estate for the benefit of your spouse/ family. The executors will have wide powers, not only in relation to the management of the assets of the trust, but also in relation to the timing and manner in which those assets are distributed. However, you can leave them a **Letter of Wishes** to follow which includes putting in place a particular inheritance tax (IHT) planning scheme. As this letter is not legally binding upon the trustees, circumstances may arise under which they consider, quite properly, that to follow it would be inappropriate, i.e. the law changes and the scheme isn't worth implementing.

PERSONAL ITEMS

Apart from major assets such as a house, there may well be relatively minor items to deal with as part of your estate. Let's say you have actually made specific bequests of valuable personal items to beneficiaries in your will. If you change your mind, you will have the expense of then redrafting clauses in your will. Alternatively, you can draft a letter of wishes outlining what you would like to see happen and lay this alongside your will (but not attached to it). Of course, using a letter of wishes (not your will) to make bequests can lead to problems if there is a dispute, because the letter isn't a legally binding document.

The advantage of this for IHT is that your executors might then be able to include these items in household and personal effects (at one third of insurance value) as part of your estate rather than drawing them to the attention of HMRC in the will for separate evaluation for IHT. HMRC does not get to see the letter of wishes, only the will!

LETTER OF WISHES

LETTER OF WISHES

Dated ....*(insert date)*

To: The Trustees of my Will

By my Will, I have appointed you as my Trustees and have left you the whole or part of my estate to hold in Discretionary Trusts for the benefit of my wife/husband* and family. My Will gives you wide powers not only in relation to the management of the assets of the Trust Fund, but also in relation to the timing and manner in which those assets are distributed.

This letter is not legally binding upon you. Circumstances may arise under which you consider, quite properly, that to follow strictly this letter of wishes would be inappropriate.

*1. During the lifetime of my wife/husband**
Whilst my wife/husband* is alive I wish you to regard her/him* as the principal beneficiary, ensuring so far as is possible that her/his* wishes are observed and her/his* welfare regarded as being of paramount importance. Subject to my wife's/husband's* wishes and welfare, I would want you to exercise your powers in such a way as will secure the least amount of tax being payable on my wife's/husband's* death.

*2. After the death of my wife/husband**
After the death of the survivor of me and my wife/husband*, I should like you to divide the Trust Fund equally between my children as and when they each attain the age of ....*(insert age)*.

Once a child reaches ... *(insert age)*, I would expect you to distribute her/his* share outright. However, there may be circumstances justifying the postponement of a distribution beyond the age of ... *(insert age)*, for example, the child may be a party to an unstable marriage, may be embarking on a risky business venture or may wish her/his* share to be retained in Trust for the benefit of her/his* children, thereby mitigating the impact of inheritance tax, income tax or capital gains tax.

Whilst any of my children are between the age of ....*(insert age range)*, I should be quite happy to see the income from their respective shares of the Trust Fund distributed to them.

Death of child
If any of my children should fail to attain the age of ... *(insert age)*, but have children of their own, then I would expect that my deceased child's share would be retained on Trust for the benefit of his/her* children when they, in turn, reach ... *(insert age)* and the share treated much in the same way as their deceased parent's share (as mentioned above).

In the event of my wife/husband* and all my children (and any children they may have) dying before the Trust Fund has been fully distributed, then I would expect you to distribute the Trust Fund as follows: ... *(insert details of how you would like the Trust Fund distributed).*

I reserve the right to revoke or vary these wishes.

Signed: ....

Dated: ....

* delete as appropriate

Loan waiver deed

If you lend someone money and later write to them releasing the debt, it will still remain part of your estate for inheritance tax purposes. To be valid, the release must be contained in a deed and properly witnessed.

REDUCE YOUR ESTATE

Where a loan is made between individuals, e.g. parent to child, HMRC will not accept that it has been waived and the estate of the lender reduced, unless the waiver is effected by deed. Use our **Loan Waiver Deed** to show HMRC that you don't wish this amount to be taken into consideration when calculating the value of your estate.

LOAN WAIVER DEED

THIS DEED is made by:

(1) "Father" ......*(insert name)* of ......*(insert address)*

(2) "Son" ......*(insert name)* of ......*(insert address)*

Recitals

A. Son is indebted to Father for the loan, brief details of which are set out in the schedule below ("the Loan").

B. By this waiver Father intends to utilise the annual exemption available to him under s.19 of **Inheritance Tax Act 1984**.

Waiver

1. Father waives and releases in favour of Son Three Thousand pounds (£3,000) of the Loan.

2. The continuing balance of the indebtedness due under the Loan following this waiver is set out in part 2 of the schedule.

<u>The Schedule</u>

Part 1 - ......*(insert details of the Loan)*

Part 2 - balance now ..... *(insert amount)*

EXECUTED AS A DEED

and DELIVERED on .... *(insert date)*

by .... *(signature of father)*

in the presence of .... *(signature of witness)*

Witness's full name..

Witness's address..

Note: "Father" can be replaced with "Mother"
"Son" can be replaced with "Daughter"

Lottery syndicate agreement

Are you in a lottery syndicate? Did you know that any winnings (football pools, National Lottery etc.) by the syndicate leader are potentially chargeable to inheritance tax as part of their estate? So what do you need to put in place before the big win?

PROTECT THE SYNDICATE LEADER

The good news is that as long as a simple agreement is in existence (and drawn up before the big win!) any winnings by the syndicate are not chargeable to inheritance tax as part of the leader's estate. The prior agreement can be verbal or written but we recommend that a written record is made, such as our **Lottery Syndicate Agreement**. (It's not necessary to lodge this with HMRC Trusts & Estates (formerly the Capital Taxes Office)).

LOTTERY SYNDICATE AGREEMENT

We, the parties hereunder, contributing (equal) amounts on a weekly/monthly/yearly* basis to the syndicate hereby confirm that the winnings from such a game of chance will be distributed in equal/proportionate* shares to the stake contributed by each individual member as shown below/in the accompanying schedule*. Such stakes/contributions applied in the purchase of such tickets or the winnings arising therefrom and distributed by the appointed manager in accordance with the agreed shares shall not be a gift within Inheritance Taxes Act 1984 section 2, but shall be treated as having no liability to inheritance tax in accordance with HMRC Statement of Practice E14. The above shall apply to the members of this syndicate including the appointed manager being the first member named below:

Syndicate member	Stake/contribution	% share of prize	Date
(1) Lisa Woods	£1 a week/month/year	50%	23 July 2014
(Signed)			
(Address)			
(2) Penny Sand	£1 a week/month/year	50%	23 July 2014
(Signed)			
(Address)			

(*) Delete as appropriate

Option to buy/sell shares clause

In the event of the untimely death of one of the director shareholders, the surviving shareholders won't want share ownership to go to someone they'd rather not be in business with. You'll need to set this condition down in writing as soon as possible. However, if you don't get the wording right, the outgoing director's estate could end up with an unexpected tax bill. What do you need to change?

SHAREHOLDERS' AGREEMENT

If there is already a shareholders' agreement, you can insert standard clauses which say that, in the event of a director shareholder dying, their personal representatives are obliged to sell and the other shareholders are obliged to buy, the deceased's shares. The price will be fixed by a specified formula, presided over by the company's auditor in case of a dispute and the funds for the purchase are often provided by appropriate life insurance policies.

HMRC's prevailing view of this is that it represents a binding contract for the sale of the property (shares) in question at the time of the transferor's death. This means that 100% business property relief (BPR) from inheritance tax is not available on the deceased's shares. This interpretation of the legislation has not yet been ratified by the courts (no case has been brought) so you could challenge this view. However, it's not worth incurring the costs because there's a much simpler solution. Grant buy and sell options instead. Because an option for tax purposes doesn't exist when it is granted but when it is exercised, it can't be held to be an existing binding contract.

Make sure you have an up-to-date shareholders' agreement in place with an **Option to Buy/Sell Shares Clause**. This should: **(1)** grant the personal representatives of the deceased shareholder an "option to sell" shares; and **(2)** grant the surviving shareholders an "option to buy" shares. This "option" argument would also work for partnership interests.

OPTION TO BUY/SELL SHARES CLAUSE

Transfer of shares

1. A shareholder shall give notice in writing (hereinafter called "the transfer notice") to the Company that they desire to transfer their share(s). Such notice shall grant an option for the Company to act as their agent for the sale of the share to the Company, or in the event of the Company not opting to purchase, to any member of the Company, or in the event of any share not being taken up, to any person selected by the Directors as one whom it is desirable in the interests of the Company to admit to membership at the fair value to be fixed by the Auditor for the time being of the Company.

2. If the Company, within the space of 56 days after being served with such transfer notice, shall elect to purchase, or shall find a member or persons selected as aforesaid willing to purchase the share (hereinafter called "the purchaser"), and give notice thereof to the proposing transferor, they shall be bound upon payment of the fair value, to transfer the share to the Company or to the purchaser who shall be bound to complete the purchase within 14 days from the service of such last-mentioned notice.

3. The executors or administrators of any deceased member shall have an option, at any time after the expiration of six months from the date of death, if and when called upon by the Directors so to do, to grant an option to buy all the shares registered in the name of the deceased member at the date of their death, or such of the same as still remain so registered, and should such executors or administrators fail to give such transfer notice within a period of 14 days after being so called upon, or should there be no such executors or administrators at the expiration of such period of six months, a transfer notice shall be deemed to have been given.

Record of gifts

One weapon in the battle to minimise inheritance tax bills is to simply give away as much as possible while you are still alive. Indeed there is even an annual tax exemption to encourage you to do just this. Keeping a record of the gifts you've made and the exemptions claimed will help your executors ward off any queries from HMRC.

KEEP A RECORD

To help your executors it's well worth keeping a **Record of Gifts** detailing dates, amounts and beneficiaries. Keep your records with your will and update them annually - perhaps a good time to do so is when you complete your tax return. There is no need to tell HMRC what you've done. It'll be up to your executors to submit the details when dealing with your estate. Retaining supporting evidence of your income, e.g. copies of tax returns, and outgoings, e.g. bank statements, would also help your executors.

RECORD OF GIFTS

Date of gift (Note 1)	Name and relationship of recipient and description of assets	Value at date of gift (£)	Amount and type of exemption claimed (Note 2)	Net value after exemptions (£)

Notes

1. Cheques are gifted on payment (not when cheque is received), i.e. the gift remains incomplete until the cheque is cleared by the paying bank.

2. The following are exempt from IHT:

(1) Gifts made between spouses.

(2) Gifts made seven years or more before death.

(3) Gifts made out of income other than capital.

(4) Gifts of up to £250 per person per tax year.

(5) Gifts to charities, political parties, housing associations and for the benefit the nation (such as works of art to a museum, or properties to the National Trust).

(6) Gifts on marriage (£5,000 per parent, £2,500 from grandparent or great grandparent and £1,000 from anyone else).

(7) Up to £3,000 per tax year to a single individual (£6,000 if you haven't used the previous year's allowance).

Notice of severance of joint tenancy

Investing in a property jointly can have significant tax savings. However, if one of you dies, your half automatically passes to the other before any will comes into effect. How can you make sure your share goes where you want it to?

AUTOMATIC TRANSFER

Most couples that jointly own a home assume they own half each. This is rarely true. In almost all cases, homes are owned under what is called joint tenancy. This means that if one of you dies, your half automatically passes to the other before any will comes into effect and therefore cannot be considered to be part of your estate. To get around this you must sever the joint tenancy and replace it with a tenancy in common. You can use our **Notice of Severance of Joint Tenancy** document for the first part of this process.

NOTICE OF SEVERANCE OF JOINT TENANCY

From: .... *(insert name 1)*

Of: .... *(insert address)*

To: .... *(insert name 2)*

Of: .... *(insert address)*

Property: .... *(insert property details)*

Title number: .... *(insert land registry title number)*

Notice

I ...... *(insert name 1)*, now give you notice terminating with immediate effect our joint tenancy in the property so that the property will be held by us as tenants-in-common in:

.... *(insert details, e.g. the following shares, namely 30% held for you and 70% held for me, or equal shares; shares yet to be decided).*

I request you to acknowledge receipt of this notice by signing and returning the duplicate notice and application enclosed.

Dated: ....*(insert date)*

Signed: ....*(insert signature of name 1)*

Enc

Receipt of notice

I ………………. *(insert name 2)*, now acknowledge receipt of the notice of which this is a copy.

I [do accept/do not accept/make no comment on*] the apportionment of the shares in the beneficial estate described above. I understand that the joint tenancy has been severed.

Dated: ……………………………………*(insert date)*

Signed: …………………………………*(insert signature of name 2)*

* delete as necessary

Application for restriction

We ………………... *(insert name 1 and name 2)* now apply to the Registrar for a restriction to be entered against the title to the property as follows:

"Except under an order of the Registrar or of the court, no disposition by a sole proprietor of the land (not being a trust corporation) under which the capital money arises is to be registered."

Dated: ……………………………………*(insert date)*

Signed: …………………………………*(insert signature of name 1)*

Dated: ……………………………………*(insert date)*

Signed: ………………………………… *(insert signature of name 2)*

Surplus income letter

In addition to a record of gifts, make a written record of what you intend to do in order to demonstrate to HMRC a "pattern of giving" out of surplus income.

WRITE A LETTER

Keep this **Surplus Income Letter** with your will to help your executors when dealing with your estate (see **Inheritance Tax Manual IHTM14242**).

SURPLUS INCOME LETTER

HMRC

....*(insert address)*
....
....
....

....*(insert date)*

Dear Sirs

This is to record that from the date of this letter it is my intention to make regular gifts, in each year ended 5 April, out of my income that, taking one year with another, is surplus to my needs. I further record that after making such gifts I will be left with sufficient income to maintain my usual standard of living.

Yours faithfully

....*(insert signature)*

Surplus income record

There is a legal exemption which excludes from inheritance tax, monetary gifts made out of your surplus income before death. How do the executors of your estate prove this surplus income tag after you've gone?

GIFTS FROM INCOME

There is no financial ceiling or percentage restriction which might otherwise limit the amount you could give away. Any money expended on gifts out of surplus income is in addition to the annual exempt amount of £3,000 and other exemptions.

If you decide to go down this route, you should make a record of your income and outgoings in sufficient detail to evidence the surplus income. Complete our **Surplus Income Record** each tax year so that the executors will be able to rebuff any challenge from HMRC over gifts made out of your income and write a letter recording your intentions. (Keep all of this with your will and record of gifts.)

SURPLUS INCOME RECORD

	TAX YEAR (5 April to 6 April)						
	1 2014/15 £	2 2015/16 £	3 2016/17 £	4 2017/18 £	5 2018/19 £	6 2019/20 £	7 2020/21 £
Income							
Salary							
State pension							
Other pensions							
Tax credits							
Dividends							
Rent (less expenses)							
Interest							
Other investment income (specify)							
Other income							
Total income							
Expenditure							
Mortgage/rent							
Household bills							
Living expenses							

	TAX YEAR (5 April to 6 April)						
	1 2014/15 £	2 2015/16 £	3 2016/17 £	4 2017/18 £	5 2018/19 £	6 2019/20 £	7 2020/21 £
Nursing home fees							
School fees							
Medical insurance							
Tax paid							
Other expenditure							
Total expenditure							
Surplus of income over expenditure							
Regular gifts (specify) e.g. cash to son							
Surplus after gifts							

Tenancy-in-common declaration

You may need a tenancy-in-common declaration for a variety of reasons. Use it as evidence to satisfy HMRC that the property is now actually owned in unequal proportions.

SPLIT TO YOUR NEEDS

A **Tenancy-in-common Declaration** is usually used when you would like to change the proportion of ownership from an automatic 50:50 split under a joint tenancy. Therefore if you sever a joint tenancy you will need to use this document instead.

This declaration should also be used if you are using a deed of gift to share out your property for inheritance tax reasons - perhaps you would like to give a third to your partner, not previously named on the deeds? Use this declaration to set out the percentage of ownership.

TENANCY-IN-COMMON DECLARATION

THIS DECLARATION OF TRUST is made the ....*(insert day)* day of ....*(insert month and year)*

BETWEEN

(1) .... *(insert your name)*

(2) ....*(insert your spouse's/partner's name)*

NOW THIS DEED WITNESSES as follows:

1. Percentage holding

It is declared that the property at ... *(insert address)* is held in the following percentages:

.... *(insert your name)* .... *(insert percentage holding)*

.... *(insert your spouse's/partner's name)* .... *(insert percentage holding)*

[2. Mortgage

For as long as there is a mortgage on the property, this deed provides that it be paid off before the sale proceeds are divided in the above percentages.]

3. Right of pre-emption

If one party to this trust wishes to sell the property they should first give notice of this intention to the other party who would have the right to buy that person's share at market value.

SIGNED AND DELIVERED AS A DEED by:

....
(insert your name)   *(insert your spouse's/partner's name)*

WITNESSED by: SIGNED by:

....
(insert witness's name)   *(insert witness's signature and address)*

Trading status report

Business property relief is available on shares in unquoted companies if certain conditions are met. This means 100% of the market value of those shares will escape inheritance tax. However, HMRC can take this relief away if the business consists "wholly or mainly" of non-trading activities such as holding investments. How should you set about persuading him otherwise?

WHOLLY OR MAINLY

When considering this test, HMRC guidance is that its interpretation of this is literal, i.e. a 51% test. This will be applied not only to turnover/profits but all aspects of the business such as capital employed, time spent by directors and employees, etc. It's particularly important where a business has several different sources of income.

For example, in **Farmer v IRC 1999** only a small part of the farm was rented out, but the rental income (investment not business) was significant in relation to the farm's income. The particular features considered in the Farmer case were: **(1)** the overall context of the business; **(2)** capital employed; **(3)** employee time; **(4)** turnover; and **(5)** profits. The only test which suggested that the let property activity was substantial was profits. Since four out of the five tests supported the view that, looking at the business as a whole, the business consisted mainly of farming activities, the claim for business property relief (BPR) was allowed.

EXCEPTED ASSETS

BPR will also be lost to the extent that the value of the shares in a company is attributable to "excepted assets". Assets will be excepted assets if they meet either of two tests:

- **"Past use" test.** The asset was not used wholly or mainly for business purposes throughout the whole of the last two years of the relevant period (broadly, the period between date of ownership and transfer of the shares, s.112(5)).

- **"Future use" test.** The asset is not required for future use in the business.In considering whether the cash is required for future use, it's not sufficient to be holding the cash speculatively for unspecified future projects, there needs to be a clear earmarked purpose for it. As with most things HMRC are wont to query, good documentation, minutes of meetings, etc. will assist with putting a case together in this respect.

Use our **Trading Status Report** board minutes to make it clear to HMRC why 100% BPR should still apply to these shares.

TRADING STATUS REPORT

Company: ....*(insert company name)*

Period covered by this report ....*(insert period covered)*

Reason for this report

The directors of .... *(insert company name)* were asked by the Company's tax advisors to consider whether there was any uncertainty about the Company's status as a trading company. Specifically [(for inheritance tax business property relief purposes) whether the company's activities were wholly or mainly trading*] or [(for capital gains tax purposes) whether or not non-trading activities were substantial*]. In reaching their conclusion a number of factors were considered (using guidance in Tax Bulletins 53 and 63, and the cases of Farmer v CIR (1999) and CIR v George (2004)) by the directors. These were as follows:

1. Turnover

(For example: "The Company owns an investment property. The receipts from the letting are not substantial* in comparison to its combined trading and letting receipts. On this measure in isolation, the company is a trading company.)

2. The asset base of the company

The value ..... *(insert figure)* of the Company's non-trading assets .... *(specify, e.g. investment property, surplus cash)* is not significant in comparison with its total assets ..... *(insert figure)*. Again, this basis alone points to the Company being a trading company. [Retention of ..... *(insert description of the asset)* previously used for the purposes of the trade was still considered to be a trading activity by the directors.] [The directors also considered it appropriate to take into account intangible assets not shown on the balance sheet when arriving at a figure for the company's total assets. For example, a figure for ....*(insert description of intangible asset, e.g. goodwill)* of ..... *(insert figure)* has been added to the Company's balance sheet for the purposes of this exercise.] [The directors also considered it appropriate to use the current market values rather than book values of other assets ..... *(specify assets)*].

[What appeared to be excessive cash balances are no longer a concern when the other balance sheet assets have been shown at their current market values. This of course includes intangible fixed assets such as goodwill, which did not appear in the balance sheet of the original financial statements of the Company.] [The directors also noted that the cash represents undrawn trading profits, which could have been paid out as salary or dividends in previous years; not the sale proceeds from the sale of an investment which had not been taken out of the Company.][The cash balances are required for a .... *(specify a clear earmarked purpose for holding the cash).*]

3. Expenses incurred/time spent by the officers and employees of the Company

On average only ..... *(insert figure)* of the Company's total expenses have been incurred on non-trading activities. This proportion is not substantial*.

The company has not and does not devote a substantial* amount of its staff resources, measured by time or in costs incurred, to non-trading activities.

4. The Company's history

The company's history is relevant to any discussion on trading status. (For example, we noted in reviewing the company's accounts that in ....*(specify accounting period)* certain receipts were substantial* to total receipts, but if looked at on a longer timescale, they may not be substantial* compared to other receipts over a longer period. Looked at in this context, therefore, the directors are able to conclude that the Company was a trading company over the period ... *(specify from when to when)*, even though that period included particular points in time when ..... *(describe measure, e.g. non-trade receipts)* amounted to a substantial* proportion of total ......*(describe measure e.g. total receipts)*.

Conclusion

[Some indicators point in one direction and others the opposite way]. We have weighed up the impact of each measure and using the history of the company over ... (*specify the period, e.g. the last five years*) as the overriding context, ... *(specify the period, e.g. of the last five years)* confirm that there is no uncertainty about the trading status of the company.

....*(insert signature)*

....*(insert position in the company)*

....*(insert date)*

Note

* *Depending on which tax then "substantial" means; (1) over 50% (i.e. wholly and mainly) for inheritance tax business property relief; or (2) 20% and over for capital gains tax.*

Transferable nil rate band checklist

When one spouse dies before the other, any unsued nil rate band can be transferred to their surviving spouse. But HMRC will require details of the inheritance tax history of the first death in order to agree any claim on the second.

TRANSFERABLE NIL RATE BAND

In October 2007 the government introduced new rules which allows a deceased's personal representatives (executors) etc. to claim all or part of the nil rate band (NRB) from their spouse or civil partner. The amount that can be claimed is the proportion that was unused when the first spouse or civil partner died. This allowable portion is known as the transferable nil rate band (TNRB).

The amount of the TNRB that can be claimed when the second spouse dies is calculated using the following formula:

% of NRB unused on first death x value of the NRB on the second death

The amount available is restricted to 100% of the NRB on the second death. This restriction is to take account of fluctuations in the level of NRBs across different tax years. This means that the level of the NRB that was in force when the first spouse died is irrelevant; it's the proportion that was unused that counts.

Example

The NRB for 2002/3 is £250,000. Danielle died in June 2002, the net value of all her assets and liabilities on death is £300,000. She leaves her entire estate to her husband George. Because this is a transfer to a spouse it's covered by the spousal gift exemption meaning that none of the £250,000 NRB available is used.

George dies in December 2014 with an estate of £700,000. The NRB for 2014/15 is £325,000.

Because Danielle left everything to George, she didn't use any of her NRB. George's personal representatives can claim £325,000 TNRB, 100% of the NRB when George dies. Therefore, the total amount of NRB that can be applied to George's estate is £650,000.

KEEP A RECORD

As there may be a considerable period of time between the first and second deaths, it may be difficult to prove what, if any, nil rate band has been transferred. Use our **Transferable Nil Rate Band Checklist** to ensure you retain all the relevant documents and records to claim the TNRB.

TRANSFERABLE NIL RATE BAND CHECKLIST

Document or record	Notes and references to supporting evidence on file
Copy of IHT forms or full written details of the assets in the estate and their values	
Death certificate	
Marriage or civil partnership certificate	
Copy of the grant of representation ("confirmation" in Scotland)	
Copy of the will (if there was one)	
A note of how the estate was passed (if there was no will)	
A copy of any deed of variation	
Probate valuations of assets that passed under the will or intestacy other than to the surviving spouse or civil partner	
Date and value of any chargeable lifetime transfers, e.g. transfers into trusts	
Date and value of any gifts made by the first spouse in the seven years prior to death	
Evidence to support the availability of IHT relief, e.g. business property relief, where the relievable assets pass to someone other then the surviving spouse or civil partner.	

Keep these documents with your own will.

Section 8

Profit extraction

Annual certificate of interest

When you receive interest on your savings from a bank or building society it will issue an annual certificate of interest to help you put the correct entries on your tax return. If your company has paid you interest for lending it money, e.g. keeping a credit balance on your director's loan account, then why shouldn't it also issue you with an annual certificate?

HELP WITH TAX AFFAIRS

The interest can be paid or credited to the director's loan account on a regular basis to be drawn against later. Generally, the company has to deduct income tax at the rate of 20% from interest paid to the director. The company has to tell HMRC how much interest it has paid each quarter (using a Form CT61) and pay over any tax deducted. This form needs to be completed and submitted to HMRC within 14 days of the quarters that end on 31 March, 30 June, 30 September and 31 December. So quarterly is probably a convenient time to put the transaction through the company's books.

In order to help the director with their tax affairs at the end of the tax year the company issues an **Annual Certificate of Interest**.

ANNUAL CERTIFICATE OF INTEREST

.... *(insert company name)*
...................................*(insert company address)*
....
....

....*(insert name of director)*
....*(insert address of director)*
....
....
....

....*(insert date)*

Dear ....*(insert name of director)*

Interest Certificate for the period 6 April ... *(insert year)* **to 5 April** ... *(insert year)*

Below is the interest you earned for the last tax year, which was paid to you or credited to your loan account.

Interest before tax   £ .... *(insert figure)*
(Gross Interest)

Tax paid   £ .... *(insert figure)*

Interest after tax   £ .... *(insert figure)*
(Net interest)

Please note that any tax deducted was paid direct to HMRC. The amount of interest actually paid to you or added to your account was the interest after tax.

Tax return. Remember to keep this certificate with your tax records. It supports interest entries you make on your self-assessment tax return.

Yours sincerely

....*(insert signature)*
[Company secretary/director]

On behalf of ....*(insert company name)*

Benefit in kind paperwork

You can get your company to pay for certain personal expenses and get a tax deduction for it if you include it as part of your negotiated remuneration package. What paperwork do you need on file to support this?

PART OF YOUR PAY PACKAGE

If your company pays, say, for a room in your house to be decorated, what documentation do you need to make sure it gets a tax deduction for this as a legitimate part of your remuneration package? Firstly, you'll need to get formal **Benefit in Kind Paperwork** drawn up which demonstrates to HMRC that the benefit was agreed by the company as a way of rewarding you for your services to the company. There is no need for any special wording, just a statement of the facts as a record for future reference. Secondly, because this is a variation of your remuneration package, you will need to incorporate it into your contract of employment by way of an addendum to the main contract. Thirdly, getting the provider of the service to invoice the company will make it absolutely clear that the liability for payment belongs with the company and not you. And fourthly, although there are no special disclosure requirements, if you include the charge for the service to remuneration costs, it reinforces your position that it's part of your pay package.

BENEFIT IN KIND PAPERWORK

1. **The board minute.** Remember that any expense charged in the Company's accounts has to meet the "wholly and exclusively" test for the purpose of the trade. Getting a formal board minute drawn up demonstrates to HMRC that the benefit was agreed on by the Company as a way of rewarding you for your services. There is no need for any special wording, just a statement of the facts as a record for future reference.

    Example:

    "Meeting of the Board of Directors of XYZ Limited on …… (insert date and time) …………. (insert location).

    It was resolved that the Company approve the payment of Mr X's …… (insert details) as part of his remuneration package.

    This award has been made in recognition of his continuing contribution to the success of the company.

    Signed ………….. (insert name) company secretary"

2. **Your contract of employment.** Because this is a variation to your remuneration package you will need to incorporate it into your contract of employment by way of an addendum.

    Example:

    "As of ……. (insert date) the Company will contract and pay for ………………………. (insert details) subject to the availability of funds. This benefit in kind is to be treated as part of your remuneration package with the Company."

Director's loan account record

A taxable benefit in kind may arise where a director is provided with a loan, either interest free or at a rate of interest below HMRC's official rate (3.25% for 2014/15). Use this document to calculate what, if anything, you need to declare to HMRC.

MAKE A NOTE

Where a cheap rate or interest-free loan is no more than £10,000 at any time during a tax year, there is no taxable benefit. But where it exceeds this the whole loan is subject to the benefits tax rules. It's therefore important to monitor loans to ensure that they don't go over the limit, so complete a record for all loans taken out by employees and directors.

Note. All loans made to the director by the company must be added together to check whether the £10,000 (for 2014/15 onwards) limit is exceeded.

DIRECTOR'S LOAN ACCOUNT RECORD

Company name: ....

Director's name: ....

Subject: *Record of transactions going through my director's loan account*

Date of transaction	Description of the transaction	Amount in ("+") £0.00	Amount out ("-") £0.00	Balance £0.00
X	Final dividend voted			
X	Interim dividend proposed			
X	Loan account interest due			
X	Expenses claim received			
X	Payment of expenses			

Director's loan account write-off letter

An overdrawn director's loan account can be cleared by the company if the directors or shareholders agree to write the loan off. However, it must get the paperwork right.

REPORTING REQUIREMENTS

Where a director or shareholder's loan is written off, s.415 of the **Income Tax (Trading and Other Income) Act 2005** says that it's taxed as income in the same way as a dividend. The director must report the write-off in their self-assessment personal tax return and the company notify the HMRC office handling its tax.

A record of the write-off should be kept by the company and the director shareholder; you can use our letter to do this and notify HMRC of the transaction.

DIRECTOR'S LOAN ACCOUNT
WRITE-OFF LETTER

....*(insert date)*

HMRC

....*(insert company's tax office)*

Dear Sirs

.... *(insert company name)* *(insert tax reference)*

On ....*(insert date)*, the company discharged loans it had made to one of its directors, ... *(insert name and address of the director),* who is also a shareholder in the above named company.

The amount of the loan discharged and written-off in the company's records was £.....*(enter the amount of the loan written off)*.

Yours faithfully

....*(insert signature)*

.... *(insert company name)*

Director's loan agreement

A director shareholder doesn't have to sign a loan agreement when they borrow money from their company. The terms of borrowing can be agreed orally or just implied. However, in certain situations a director is required by company law to obtain permission from the shareholders prior to borrowing company money.

GET IT IN WRITING

Shareholder approval (generally by ordinary resolution) is only required for directors' loans in excess of £10,000 (the limit is £50,000 if the loan is to meet expenditure on company business). But in all situations where a company lends money to a director we recommend that a written agreement setting out the key terms should be drawn up. Apart from anything else it will help prove the existence of a loan where HMRC makes enquiries.

Use and modify as needed our sample loan agreement for all company to director loans.

DIRECTOR'S LOAN AGREEMENT

THIS AGREEMENT is made on ....*(insert date)*

BETWEEN

(1).. *(insert name of company)*
of .... *(insert address of company)* ("the Lender"); and

(2) ....*(insert name of director)*
of ....*(insert address of director)* (the "Borrower").

The Lender has been requested to make a loan to the Borrower which the Lender has agreed to do upon the terms and conditions which follow.

1. Amount of loan

The Lender will lend to the Borrower and the Borrower will borrow from the Lender the outstanding balance on the Borrower's loan account with the Lender ("the Loan") on the terms which follow.

2. Interest

The Borrower shall pay to the Lender interest on the Loan at the rate of [NIL%] ...... *(insert figure)*] per annum quarterly on the last day of each of the months of [March, June, September and December] [January, April, July and October] [February, May, August and November] in each year. The first such payment to be made on whichever of the interest payment dates first occurs after the advance of the Loan and to be in respect of the period from and including the date of such advance until the next interest payment date.

3. Repayment

Unless otherwise agreed, the Borrower may only repay the Loan by a single payment on .... *(insert date)*.

4. Compulsory repayment subject to demand

The Lender may, by notice in writing to the Borrower, demand the immediate payment of all moneys due or incurred by the Borrower to the Lender together with all interest and any other sums forthwith (or otherwise as the Lender may require) at any time if the Borrower does not pay on the due date any money which may have become due hereunder or under any document supplemental hereto.

5. Compulsory repayment without demand

All moneys and obligations due or incurred by the Borrower to the Lender shall become immediately due and payable on the happening of any of the following events:

(a) the death or bankruptcy of the Borrower;

(b) if a petition is presented for an administration order to be made in relation to the Borrower pursuant to the **Insolvency Act 1986**;

(c) if any secured creditor or encumbrancer takes possession or a receiver (which expression shall include an administrative receiver as defined by the Insolvency Act 1986) is appointed of all or any part of the property and assets of the Borrower.

6. Interpretation

Covenants, warranties and undertakings given by an individual shall be binding on his personal representatives and executors.

7. Governing law

The Law of England shall apply to this Loan and the parties submit to the jurisdiction of the English courts.

EXECUTED as a deed on the day and year first above written.

EXECUTED as a DEED by)
[The Lender])
in the presence of)
Signature of witness ....
Name of witness ....
Address ....
Occupation ....

EXECUTED as a DEED by)
[The Borrower])
in the presence of)
Signature of witness ....
Name of witness ....
Address ....
Occupation ....

Distributable profits board minute

Once you've made a profit the challenge is getting it out of your company in the most tax-efficient way. Paperwork to prove you had sufficient profits to pay a dividend is essential.

A LEGAL DIVIDEND

Company law says that once you've established the availability of distributable profits you can pay a dividend. These come in two types, interim and final. The directors have the power to pay an interim dividend if the company's interim accounts show sufficient distributable (retained) profits at that time. A final dividend must be proposed by the directors and approved by the shareholders. HMRC can challenge payments described as dividends if they have not been declared and paid in accordance with company law. Indeed, if the directors allow a dividend to be paid when there are not enough retained profits it will be treated as unlawful. To record the directors' proper consideration, use our **Distributable Profits Board Minute**.

DISTRIBUTABLE PROFITS BOARD MINUTE

There was then produced to the meeting [interim] accounts. The chairperson confirmed that the interim accounts had been prepared in accordance with the Company's normal accounting policies. The directors then considered the [interim] accounts and it was noted that the amount of profits available for distribution shown was £. . . . . . *(insert figure)*.

The directors concluded that the [interim] accounts enabled them to make a reasonable judgement as to the amount of the distributable profits of the Company. It was noted that as the proposed dividend is to be paid immediately, the directors would not be required to undertake a further assessment of profitability except to the extent that were aware of any matters which might result in the Company making a loss. It was considered that there were no such matters.

The directors considered carefully the effect the dividend would have on the Company's ability to pay its debts as they fall due. To assist the directors there was produced to the meeting details of the Company's [cash flow] projections [and] [its current bank overdraft facilities]. It was noted that even after payment of the interim dividend, the Company would continue to have the resources to meet trading debts as they fell due.

Dividend voucher

One of the things you have to do when you wish to pay a dividend to the shareholders in your company is write out a record of the dividend and give it to the shareholder.

ISSUE A VOUCHER

To keep HMRC at bay, it's a good idea to issue a **Dividend Voucher** after each dividend (interim or final). An alternative to this is to have it "approved" at the next meeting so that the company secretary will only have to issue one dividend voucher at the end of each tax year.

DIVIDEND VOUCHER

. ...*(insert company name)*

....*(insert company address)*

....*(insert date)*

....*(insert shareholder's name)*

....*(insert shareholder's address)*

....

Dear ....*(insert shareholder's name)*

Dividend for the period ending .... *(insert your financial year-end)*

I give below the details of the dividend payment made to you on ....*(insert date)*.

Number of shares: ....*(insert number of shares)* Ordinary (or, if other, specify type) shares of .... *(insert nominal value)* each.

Dividend rate: ....*(insert percentage or pence per share)*

Total dividend payable for the period ending ....
(insert date): .... *(insert figure)*

Total tax credit: £ .... *(insert figure)*

Note. Tax credit is dividend paid x 10/90, e.g. on £900 the tax credit would be £100. You don't have to do anything with this other than record it on the voucher.

Remember to keep this voucher with your tax records. It supports the dividend entries you make on your self assessment tax return.

Yours sincerely

On behalf of ....*(insert company name)*

....*(insert signature)*
[Company secretary/director]

Dividend waiver

Broadly, a dividend waiver involves a shareholder waiving their entitlement to the dividend before the right to it has accrued. A dividend waiver can therefore be used as a way of reducing the income a higher rate tax-paying shareholder receives from the company. However, the timing of the document is crucial.

No DIVIDEND, THANK YOU

When a company pays a dividend, all the shareholders receive a cheque in proportion to their shareholding in the company. It's a case of all or nothing. Plus, under present rules, anyone liable to the higher rate of tax suffers an additional income tax on dividends. In other words, if you are already a higher rate taxpayer the problem with taking an extra dividend is that you pay tax on it. Yet fellow shareholders may have no tax to pay. This is where dividend waivers come in.

They can therefore be used as a method of reducing the income a shareholder receives from the company. You cannot waive the dividend after you obtain the right to receive it. Use our **Dividend Waiver** agreement to achieve this.

One possible use of a dividend waiver would be to divert income to one or more of the other shareholders. However, HMRC clearly states in its manuals that it will look very closely at dividend waivers where the non-waiving shareholder would pay less tax on the dividend than the waiving shareholder. Therefore, it's best to state in the deed of waiver that it has been made to allow the company to retain funds for a specific purpose. Also make sure the dividend declared per share times the total number of shares in issue before any waivers does not exceed the amount of the company's distributable reserves.

A waiver of dividends within twelve months before any right to the dividend has accrued avoids a possible inheritance tax problem (s.15 of the **Inheritance Tax Act 1984**). This is another good reason for the period of 364 days mentioned on the waiver.

DIVIDEND WAIVER

By this my deed dated ………… *(insert date)*, I ….……………. *(insert full name)* hereby irrevocably waive my entitlement to (the final/interim/any)* dividend arising on my entire holding of Ordinary (or, if other, specify type) shares in . . . . . *(insert company name)* from this day for EITHER:

(A) a period of maximum: 364 (three hundred and sixty four) days,

OR

(B) based on the accounts for the period ended …………….. *(insert date)*

The purpose of this waiver is to allow the Company to retain funds for ……………. *(insert specific purpose)*.

Signed...
(Shareholder)

Full name..

In the presence of:

Signature of
Witness..

Full name..

Address..

....

Occupation ....

* delete as necessary

A deed should be prepared and reviewed by a solicitor.

Interest payable on loan account minute

Where a director's loan account is in credit rather than overdrawn, the company can agree at a board meeting to pay interest on the credit balance. This can be added as a further credit to the director's loan account or paid to them (after deducting basic rate tax).

WHEN TO USE THIS BOARD MINUTE

It's advisable to set out the terms and conditions of how much interest will be paid and when, and record this in a board minute - our **Interest Payable on Loan Account Minute** provides suitable wording. This proves that there is an obligation on the company to pay this interest.

The company is entitled to claim a tax deduction for the interest it pays on money it owes a director.

INTEREST PAYABLE ON LOAN ACCOUNT MINUTE

Board minute

The director(s) …………….. *(insert name(s))* has/have requested that the Company pay interest at a commercial rate of interest on their director's loan account when it is in credit. Having discussed the matter, the Board has resolved that the Company will pay interest on their loan account(s) at the rate of …......% *(insert figure)* above bank base rate per annum, to be credited to the loan account on the first day of each quarter based on the average balance outstanding in the previous quarter.

Interim dividend board minute

A dividend is the most tax efficient way of getting money out of your company. However, you'll need a document to prove to HMRC when the dividend was declared.

WHEN WAS IT TAKEN?

For a comprehensive board minute concerning all possible factors to be taken into account in proving that a payment to you was in fact an interim dividend see our **Interim Dividend Board Minute**.

The board minute details when the meeting took place and the total interim dividend proposed, with consideration for the distributable profits of the company and the effect the dividend would have on the company's ability to pay its debts as they fall due.

INTERIM DIVIDEND BOARD MINUTE

....(*insert name of company*) Limited

Minutes of a meeting of the board of directors of .... (*insert name of company*) Limited held at ....(*insert venue*) on ..... (*insert date*) at ..... (*insert time*).

Present	Name	Position
Apologies for absence received from	**Name**	**Position**

1. Chairperson

.... (*insert name*) was appointed chairperson of the meeting.

2. Notice and quorum

The chairperson reported that due notice of the meeting had been given and that a quorum was present. Accordingly, the chairperson declared the meeting open.

3. Minutes of the meeting held on

The chairperson reported that the minutes of the board meeting held on ..... (*insert date*) were correct and that no other issues arose from those minutes.

4. Proposed interim dividend

4.1.   The chairperson reported that [the meeting had been called because the Company had been requested by its shareholders to consider the payment of an interim dividend out of the profits available for distribution] [the business of the meeting was to consider, and if thought appropriate approve, the payment of an interim dividend to the shareholders of the company.]

4.2.   It was noted that the Company's Articles of Association allowed the directors to pay interim dividends [only if it appeared to them that those dividends were justified by the profits of the Company available for distribution].

5. *Proposed dividend*

5.1. The chairperson then reported that the directors being asked to consider the proposal for the Company to pay an interim dividend for year of £....*(insert figure)* per ordinary share at a total cost of £..... *(insert figure)*. If the directors resolved to pay the dividend it would be paid [immediately] to the member(s) whose names appeared on the Company's register of members at the time of the resolution.

5.2. There was then produced at the meeting a copy of the annual accounts for the Company for the period ended ..... *(insert date)* [which had been laid before the members in general meeting][had been sent to members][and contained an unqualified report from the Company's auditors].

5.3. The directors noted that the accounts showed profits available for distribution of £..... *(insert figure)*.

5.4. It was confirmed that [no dividends] [dividends in the sum of £ ..... *(insert figure)* had been paid since the balance sheet date of ..... *(insert date)*] [all the distributable profits shown in the Company's most recent annual accounts had been distributed to member(s)].

5.5. It was reported that the distributable profits of the Company as determined by the relevant items shown in the accounts [after taking into account distributions made since balance sheet date of .... *(insert date)*] were such as [would] [would not] justify the payment of an interim dividend of £ ..... *(insert figure)* proposed.

5.6. [There was then produced to the meeting [an individual profit and loss account and balance sheet showing profits, losses, assets and liabilities capital and reserves of the company as at ..... *(insert date)*] [interim accounts]. The [chairperson] [finance director] confirmed that the interim accounts had been prepared in accordance with the company's normal accounting policies [and the Company's auditors had confirmed that it was appropriate for the directors to rely on interim accounts].]

5.7. [The directors then considered the interim accounts and it was noted that the amount of profits available for distribution shown in the interim accounts was £......... *(insert figure)*. [It was explained this included ......*(insert details of anything material, for example interim dividends from subsidiaries)*.]

5.8. Having discussed the interim accounts and asked any questions, the directors concluded that the interim accounts enabled them to make a reasonable judgement both as to the £..... *(insert figure)* of the distributable profits of the Company and as to the £..... *(insert figure)* of each item to which it was their duty to have regard in determining the profits available for distribution. It was noted that as the proposed dividend is to be paid immediately, the directors would not be required to undertake a further assessment of profitability except to the extent that they were aware of any matters which might result in the company making a loss. It was considered that there were no such matters.

5.9.   The directors considered carefully the effect the dividend would have on the Company's ability to pay its debts as they fall due, having regard to the entirety of the Company's business and the actual and contingent liabilities (future and present inherent in that business). [To assist the directors there was produced to the meeting details of the Company's [cash flow] projections [and] [its current bank overdraft facilities.] [It was noted that the [finance director] had confirmed that even after payment of the interim dividend, he was of the view that the Company would continue to have the resources to meet trading debts as they fell due.]

5.10. [To further assist the directors, the chairperson reported that ..... *(insert name of holding company)* had written to the Company giving confirmation to the effect that as long as the Company remained within the ....*(insert name of holding company)* group of Companies ......*(insert name of holding company)* would use all reasonable endeavours to seek to ensure that the Company continued to be able to meet its foreseeable debts as they fall due; and if at any time the ..... *(insert name of holding company)* sold the Company to a third party it would not do so without endeavouring to obtain similar assurance from the third party concerning the Company's ability to meet foreseeable debts.]

6. Resolutions

After further discussion, it was resolved that;

6.1.   The directors, having satisfied themselves that its payment would not affect the Company's ability to pay its foreseeable debts as they fell due, a dividend of £ ....*(insert figure)* ..... *(insert figure)* pence per ordinary share at a total cost of £ ..... *(insert figure)* dividend be paid [immediately] [on ..... *(insert date)*] to the member(s) of the Company whose name(s) appear on the register of members at the time of the resolution.

6.2 . The payment of this dividend was to be satisfied using the available cash resources of the Company satisfied by drawing down on ......*(insert details of any loan facility with the bank)* [and/or left outstanding on intra group loan account].

6.3.   [....
. ... directors' names)]
[The company secretary] be and hereby authorised to take all the steps necessary to ensure payment of the dividend.

7. Close

There was no further business and the chairperson declared the meeting closed.

....*(insert signature of Chairperson)*
Chairperson

.... *(insert date)*

Licence agreement (garage)

You might have already thought about charging your company for the use of your office at home. But what about situations where it is effectively using your garage as a storage facility? Can it get a tax deduction if it pays compensation for this convenience?

COMPANY STORAGE

If you have to use your own garage for company storage, can you claim rent in addition to that charged for using your home as an office? Yes. However, you will need to record any payment made to you by your company for use of your garage as such, both in your company's books (as an expense) and on your own tax return (as income). However, on your personal tax return you now get to claim for any additional costs of meeting your company's requirements for safeguarding those items (stock, records etc.) that are in your garage. Here's eight to get you started: **(1)** some products must not be exposed to high or low temperatures, so a proportion of household electricity costs to cover use of a heater (winter) or a fan (summer) in the garage should be claimed; **(2)** any storage boxes/cages; **(3)** additional insurance premiums; **(4)** security measures; **(5)** additional lighting; **(6)** weather proofing; **(7)** smoke alarm, fire extinguisher, sand bucket (particularly for chemical spills) etc.; and **(8)** the cost of a trolley to move products to and from the car/van - health and safety must be observed at all times.

Back this up with a **Licence Agreement (Garage)** between you and your company setting out the terms and conditions.

LICENCE AGREEMENT (GARAGE)

This agreement is made on .... *(insert date)* between

(1) .... *(insert company name)* (the "Company") and

(2) .... *(insert property owner's name)* (the "Property Owners")

(3) .... *(insert property owner's name)* (the "Property Owners")

It is agreed that

1. The Property Owners jointly own .... *(insert address of the property)* (the "Property").

2. The Property includes accommodation and contains an area ("the Garage Storage") which is available for use by the Company and which it is envisaged shall be used by the Company from time to time.

3. It is agreed that in consideration for its use of the Garage Storage, the Company shall pay the Property Owners rent. This rent is to take account of a proportion of the Property Owners' expenses incurred in providing it, as is fairly attributable to the use of the Garage Storage by the Company including (but not limited to) a proportion of mortgage interest, insurance, heating and lighting costs, maintenance and repair. The proportion is to be agreed between the parties from time to time having regard to the actual use made by the Company of the Garage Storage.

4. The Property Owners to take such steps as are necessary for the items stored not to be exposed to extremes of temperature whilst within the Garage Storage.

5. The Property Owners to put suitable security and fire prevention measures in place to reduce the risk of loss of items held in the Garage Storage.

6. The Property Owners to put such procedures in place that will allow the Garage Storage to comply with the Company's health and safety policy.

Signed on behalf of the Company ....

Name (in capitals) ....

Position..

Signed by the Property Owners (1) ....

Signed by the Property Owners (2) ....

Date ....

Licence agreement

Where your company makes a payment to you in return for being allowed to use your home or other property for its business, you should draw up an agreement to formalise the arrangement.

USE AN AGREEMENT

If your company uses part of your home, e.g. for you to work from or to store stock, you can charge it rent. As long as the property is used by the company for its business, it can deduct from its profits the rent paid to you. You will be liable to pay tax on this income net of expenses so it will need to be included on your tax return.

It's sensible to set the rent at a level that at least covers your costs, but not much more than this. The arrangement should be formalised by an agreement which gives the company rights to use your property, but not rights over ownership. This is called a **Licence Agreement**.

LICENCE AGREEMENT

This agreement is made on .... *(insert date)* between

(1) .... *(insert company name)* (the "Company") and

(2) .... *(insert property owner's name)* (the "Property Owners")

(3) .... *(insert property owner's name)* (the "Property Owners")

It is agreed that

1. The Property Owners jointly own .... *(insert address of the property)* (the "Property").

2. The Property includes accommodation and contains furniture ("the Home Office") which is available for use by the Company and which it is envisaged shall be used by the Company from time to time.

3. It is agreed that in consideration for its use of the Home Office, the Company shall reimburse to the Property Owners such proportion of any expenses they incur in providing it as is fairly attributable to the use of the Home Office by the Company including (but without limitation) provision of broadband facilities, a proportion of mortgage interest, insurance, heating and lighting costs, maintenance and repair. The proportion is to be agreed between the parties from time to time having regard to the actual use made by the Company of the Home Office.

Signed on behalf of the Company ....

Name (in capitals) ....

Position..

Signed by the Property Owners (1) ....

Signed by the Property Owners (2) ....

Date ....

Spouse's job description

A business can pay a salary to the spouse or other family member of its owner if they work for it. Having a formal job description will help justify the amount paid if HMRC decides to challenge it.

How much?

The wages paid to a spouse will be a valid tax deduction for the business if HMRC is happy that they are paid at a commercial rate for the work performed. First assess exactly what your partner does for the business. Use our example of a **Spouse's Job Description** to help you record their responsibilities. Next, calculate the average number of hours spent by your spouse per week or month on business activities. This can be tricky, but even a rough diary note made at the time is good evidence should HMRC ever seek to challenge the amount paid. If your business is run through a company you should check that the gross wage you expect to pay to your spouse/partner is at least £6.50 per hour worked, which is the national minimum wage (NMW) from October 2014. Unincorporated businesses that pay family members who live at home do not have to worry about the NMW. Remember, for the business to be guaranteed a tax deduction, the wage must actually be paid rather than just made as an accounting adjustment in the books.

SPOUSE'S JOB DESCRIPTION

1. Credit control clerk

Job title	Credit control clerk
Accountability	Accounts manager
Location	Main office (at your office address)
Brief description	To maintain and monitor 150 credit accounts
Duties and responsibilities	Cash allocation on computerised system Debt collection via telephone and standard letter Liaison with debt collection agency Some attendance at county courts Attendance of local credit meetings Maintaining credit limits Processing credit applications including credit checks Liaising with sales team
Hours of work	20 hours per week (flexible overtime may be required)
Rate of pay	£6.50 per hour (minimum)

2. PA role

Job title	Personal assistant (PA)
Accountability	Managing director (MD)
Location	Main office (at your office address)
Brief description	Work closely with the MD to provide day-to-day administrative support.

Duties and responsibilities	Screening telephone calls, enquiries and requests and handling them if they do not think it necessary to pass on to their manger Organising the MD's diary Making appointments Dealing with incoming e-mail, faxes and post Taking dictation Writing letters and reports Carrying out background research into subjects the manager is dealing with, and presenting findings in an easily digestible form Standing in for the MD in their absence Organising meetings Liaising with clients, suppliers and other staff Making decisions and delegating work to others when the manager is unavailable Devising and maintaining office systems to deal efficiently with paper flow, and the organisation and storage of paperwork, documents and computer-based information Taking responsibility for recruiting and training junior staff and delegating work to them Arranging travel and accommodation Travelling with the MD from time to time, to take notes at meetings, take dictation and provide general assistance in presentations
Hours of work	20 hours per week (flexible overtime may be required)
Rate of pay	£6.50 per hour (minimum)

Year-end bonus board minute

Bonuses for employees or directors declared after the year-end may only be accrued in the balance sheet if there was a "legal or constructive obligation at the balance sheet date" to make such payments. All other bonuses declared after the year-end cannot be included in the accounts until the following year.

BEFORE THE YEAR-END

It's common tax planning to prepare a draft set of accounts, work out the tax liability and then decide to vote a bonus to the directors (which must be paid within nine months of the year-end). This bonus is then included in the accounts to either clear an overdrawn director's loan account or reduce the company's corporation tax liability.

So you'll need to get an agreement in place before the year-end to pay bonuses after the year-end so they can still be provided for in the accounts. This condition can be easily satisfied by preparing a **Year-end Bonus Board Minute** before the company's year end setting out the basis for determining it (e.g. x% of profits).

YEAR-END BONUS BOARD MINUTE

………………………………………………………….(*insert name of company*) Limited

Minutes of a meeting of the board of directors

Held at ………………………………………………………………….(*insert location*)

On ………………… (*insert date*) at …………………….. (*insert time*)

Present	Name	Position

Apologies for absence received from	Name	Position

1. Chairperson

………………………….. (*insert name*) was appointed chairperson of the meeting.

2. Notice and quorum

The chairperson reported that due notice of the meeting had been given and that a quorum was present. Accordingly, the chairperson declared the meeting open.

3. Minutes of the previous meeting

The chairperson reported that the minutes of the board meeting held on .... *(insert date)* were correct and that no other issues arose from those minutes.

4. Resolutions

It was resolved that:

4.1 The director(s) will receive a bonus based on the results of the Company at .... *(insert year-end date)*. The bonus will be calculated as .... *(insert details, e.g. as x% of profit)*.

4.2 The payment of this bonus will be made once the accounts have been finalised.

5. Close

There was no further business and the chairperson declared the meeting closed.

.... *(insert signature of Chairperson)*
Chairperson

.... *(insert date)*

Section 9

Property investment

Capital allowances checklist

Since April 2014 it has been crucial for prospective buyers of second-hand commercial buildings to ensure that the seller has allocated their expenditure on fixtures to a capital allowances pool before the sale. If they haven't, then the buyer won't be able to claim capital allowances on them. Therefore, it's important to have an up-to-date record of all expenditure on fixtures and the capital allowances claimed.

IDENTIFY THE FIXTURES

For the seller. To ensure that a building containing fixtures is readily saleable (and commands a better price), you should maintain accurate records of all your expenditure on fixtures, together with evidence that you (and all previous qualifying owners since April 2014) have pooled such expenditure. The records should include a description of the fixture, the date it was acquired, the original cost, the capital allowances claimed and the identity of the installer. Use our **Capital Allowances Checklist** to identify and record the fixtures and fittings within a building that qualify for CAs.

For the buyer. If you're buying a commercial property, you'll need to make sure the pooling requirement has been met by the seller. Provide the seller with the **Capital Allowances Checklist** so that they can identify any fixtures which they haven't claimed capital allowances on so that they can pool these prior to completion.

CAPITAL ALLOWANCES CHECKLIST

Capital allowances can only be claimed on plant and machinery and not on buildings. However, the legislation specifies those assets that, while falling under the definition of buildings, will qualify as plant. These items are listed separately under their relevant section.

Asset description	Date acquired	Installer	Original cost (£)	Capital allowances [already claimed] (£)	Sale value (£)
Electrical systems (specific to trade):					
Wiring to fixed plant					
Switchgear					
Emergency lighting					
Specialised lighting (e.g. window display)					
Other:					
Space and water heating systems					
Hot water system					
Air conditioning (including any associated suspended ceiling or floor)					
Air purification system					
Manufacturing or processing equipment (list):					

Asset description	Date acquired	Installer	Original cost (£)	Capital allowances [already claimed] (£)	Sale value (£)
Storage equipment (list):					
Cold room					
Display equipment (list):					
White goods:					
Cooker					
Washing machine					
Dishwasher					
Refrigerator					
Other:					
Sanitary fittings:					

Asset description	Date acquired	Installer	Original cost (£)	Capital allowances [already claimed] (£)	Sale value (£)
Washbasins					
Sinks					
Baths					
Showers					
Other:					
Networking systems:					
Computer network system (including wiring)					
Telephone network system (including wiring)					
Walkways:					
Lifts					
Hoists					
Escalators					

Asset description	Date acquired	Installer	Original cost (£)	Capital allowances [already claimed] (£)	Sale value (£)
Moving walkways					
Fire and security equipment:					
CCTV					
Sound insulation					
Fire alarm system					
Fire extinguishers					
Sprinkler system					
Mechanical door closers					
Other fire-fighting equipment					
Burglar alarm system					
Safe					

Asset description	Date acquired	Installer	Original cost (£)	Capital allowances [already claimed] (£)	Sale value (£)
Other:					
Fixtures and fittings:					
Moveable partitioning					
Carpets					
Removable floor coverings					
Blinds					
Curtains					
Mezzanine floor					
Trade and information signs					
Any other machinery not listed above:					

Asset description	Date acquired	Installer	Original cost (£)	Capital allowances [already claimed] (£)	Sale value (£)
TOTAL DISPOSAL VALUE					

Chattels checklist

Anything moveable is generally not considered to be part of a property and so not subject to stamp duty land tax. How can you safely use this to your advantage?

STAMP DUTY LAND TAX - CHATTELS

You have to pay stamp duty land tax (SDLT) when you buy a property over a certain price threshold. SDLT is calculated as a percentage of the purchase price of the property and is paid by the purchaser. From 20 March 2014 the rates are:

PURCHASE PRICE	SDLT RATE
Up to £125,000	Zero
Over £125,000 to £250,000	1%
Over £250,000 to £500,000	3%
Over £500,000 to £1 million	4%
Over £1 million to £2 million	5%
Over £2 million	7%

The problem is that SDLT is not a tiered system so the SDLT on a property costing £250,000 would be £2,500 (£250,000 x 1%) whereas the SDLT on a property costing just £1 more would jump to £7,500 (£250,001 x 3%). So as a buyer, you would like to keep the price under £250,000. The seller, on the other hand, doesn't have to pay SDLT, so will want to get as much as possible for their property. The solution would be for both you and the seller to come to an agreement whereby the seller prices the property below, say, the £250,000 threshold, and you pay separately for any fixtures and fittings (chattels). However, if HMRC disputes the amount attributed to the chattels, it will request a full inventory and breakdown of the consideration - so use our **Chattels Checklist** to record the value of the relevant items.

CHATTELS CHECKLIST

Chattel	Approximate market value (£)
Inside the property: Carpets	
Flooring	
Curtains	
Blinds	
Lamp shades	
Light fittings	
Mirrors	
Coat hooks and stands	
Freestanding kitchen white goods: Cooker	
Microwave	
Fridge	
Freezer	
Dishwasher	
Washing machine	
Tumble dryer	
Extractor fan	
Portable appliances: Electric fires	
Gas fires	
Fans	
Humidifier	
Other:	
Other:	
Other:	

Chattel	Approximate market value (£)
In the garden: Garden shed (and contents)	
Garden ornaments	
Plants in pots	
Flood lights	
Other:	
Other:	

Declaration of trust

If spouses or civil partners own a property jointly, HMRC will normally treat the rental income from that property as if it belonged to the parties equally. However, if one of the individuals pays tax at a lower rate than the other, it would be more beneficial to declare the income as belonging to them. To do this, you will need a declaration of trust.

JOINTLY OWNED PROPERTY

There may be situations where it is preferable for you to own a property jointly with your spouse. For example, you're both basic-rate taxpayers, but if you were the sole owner, the rental income would take you into the higher-rate band. By owning the property jointly, you can both have a share of the rental income and stay below the higher-rate band. HMRC will automatically treat you and your spouse as sharing the income 50:50 even if you don't actually own the property in equal shares. This could be a problem where you want to allocate more of the rental profits to the lower earning spouse.

However, if you don't own the property in equal proportions, you can jointly elect to be taxed on your actual shares. To do this you must both complete and sign HMRC's Form 17 (Declaration of beneficial interests in joint property and income) and send it to HMRC. To support this declaration, you will also need to send evidence that the property is actually owned in unequal proportions by signing a **Declaration of Trust**.

DECLARATION OF TRUST

THIS DECLARATION OF TRUST is made the ......*(insert day)* day of ......*(insert month and year)*

BETWEEN

(1)..*(insert your name)*

(2)..*(insert your spouse's name)*

NOW THIS DEED WITNESSES as follows:

1. Percentage holding

It is declared that the property at .... *(insert address)* is held in the following percentages:

.... *(insert your name)* .... *(insert percentage holding)*
.... *(insert your spouse's name)* .... *(insert percentage holding)*

2. Mortgage

For as long as there is a mortgage on the property, this deed provides that it be paid off before the sale proceeds are divided in the above percentages.

3. Right of pre-emption

If one party to this trust wishes to sell the property they should first give notice of this intention to the other party who would have the right to buy that person's share at market value.

SIGNED AND DELIVERED AS A DEED by:

....
(insert your signature)   *(insert your spouse's signature)*

....
(insert your name)   *(insert your spouse's name)*

WITNESSED by:

....
(insert witness's signature)

....
(insert witness's name and address)

Election for plant and machinery purchased with a building - s.198/s.199 election

More often than not, when a commercial building is sold, the seller, having made a claim for capital allowances, will ask the buyer to enter into a special tax agreement. What format should this take to satisfy HMRC?

FIXING A VALUE

From April 2012 for the buyer of a previously owned building to be able to make a claim for capital allowances (CAs) on qualifying fixtures and fittings, the seller and the buyer must invoke one of two procedures to settle the price allocated to the fixtures. The two options are:

. a joint election under the CAA 2001 s.198 (or s.199 for leases) to settle the amount of the sale price attributable to fixtures (which cannot exceed the seller's original cost); or

. where agreement on value can't be reached, an application to the First-tier Tribunal for an independent determination.

AGREED VALUE

There is no legal requirement to agree a value at the tax-written down value (original cost less CAs already claimed by the seller). Whilst this may be of benefit to the seller's tax position, as they won't have to pay tax on any overclaim of allowances, it will be a disadvantage to the buyer. The higher the agreed value for fixtures and fittings, the greater the allowances to the buyer - where the seller's tax rate is lower than the buyer's tax rate, there may be scope for the buyer to negotiate a higher disposal value by meeting the seller's tax clawback.

TIME LIMIT

The election must be made in writing within two years of the date of completion and is irrevocable.

ELECTION FOR PLANT AND MACHINERY PURCHASED WITH A BUILDING - S.198/S.199 ELECTION

Notification of an Election to use an alternative apportionment in accordance with s.198/s.199 **Capital Allowances Act 2001**, between ....(insert name of seller) and ....(insert name of buyer).

Property address:...

Interest (freehold/leasehold): ....

Seller's name and address:..

Tax district and reference:...

Buyer's name and address: ....

Tax district and reference:...

Date of completion of sale: ....

Amount apportioned to machinery and plant fixtures (£):..
(see attached for details)

Sale price (£): ....

The seller and the buyer hereby jointly elect, pursuant to the provisions of s.198/s.199 Capital Allowances Act 2001, that the amount of the sale price to be treated as capital expenditure on plant and machinery incurred by the buyer on the provision of the fixtures is ....(insert amount as above). A list of the fixtures is given on the next page.

Signed: ....

Name of Seller: ....

Date: ....

Signed: ....

Name of Buyer: ....

Date: ....

Example:

Schedule of Plant and Machinery to included in s.198 Election

.... *(insert address)*

Item	Apportioned Amount
Ventilation	£4,500.00
Blinds	£1,500.00
Total	**£6,000.00**

EXAMPLE CLAUSES FOR CONTRACT

1. In this clause "Elected Plant" means plant and/or machinery (within the meaning of the Capital Allowances Act 2001) which constitutes fixtures and on which the Seller has claimed capital allowances and in respect of which it has to bring a disposal value into its tax computations by reason of this sale.

2. The Seller and Buyer agree that the part of the Purchase Price attributable to the Elected Plant is £X

3. Within two years of completion at a time determined by the Seller and only if the Seller has made a claim for capital allowances in respect of the Elected Plant, the Seller and the Buyer will each hand the other a signed election under section 198 of the Capital Allowances Act 2001 (CAA 2001) in respect of the Elected Plant in a form as set out in Schedule [X] which will satisfy the provisions of section 201 of the Capital Allowances Act 2001.

4. The Seller and the Buyer each warrant that they will comply with their respective procedural obligations under Section 201 of the CAA 2001 in respect of the Section 198 Election.

5. The Seller warrants that the sum specified in Clause 2 and forming the joint election pursuant to section 198 of the CAA 2001 detailed in the form attached to this agreement is not greater than the amount of the capital expenditure which was treated for the purpose of the CAA 2001 as incurred by the Seller on the provision of the Elected Plant.

6. The Seller warrants that it will bring into account in the relevant accounting period a disposal value for the Elected Plant equal to the sum specified in Clause 1.2.

Election for rent-a-room relief not to apply

Where you let part of your home, HMRC calculates the taxable income for a year by deducting a fixed sum from the rent etc. you receive. This deduction is called rent-a-room relief and is currently set at £4,250. However, if your apportioned running costs are more than this, you can elect for this relief not to apply.

MAKING THE ELECTION

Where you own the property jointly this relief is halved (£2,125). And where the relief is given you are not entitled to deduct other expenses related to renting the property, e.g. mortgage interest, repairs etc.

However, you can elect for rent-a-room relief not to apply to income for a tax year. This means that instead you can claim the actual expenses you have incurred. An election would be worthwhile where your running costs (including loan or mortgage interest) for a year exceed the rent-a-room amount.

An election must be made by the second 31 January following the end of the tax year you wish it to apply for. For example, if you wanted the relief not to apply to 2014/15, you have until 31 January 2017 to make the election. You can withdraw an election within the same time limit.

A claim can be made as part of submitting your self-assessment tax return or it can be made separately, providing it is within the time limit.

ELECTION FOR RENT-A-ROOM RELIEF NOT TO APPLY

HMRC

....*(insert address)*

....

....

....

....*(insert date)*

Dear Sirs

Rent-a-room relief

....***(insert your name)***

....***(insert your ten-digit tax reference)***

In accordance with s.799 of the Income Tax Trading and Other Income Act 2005 I elect that for the year ………….. *(insert the tax year for which you want the election to apply)* rent-a-room relief shall not apply to the income I received from letting …………………………………*(insert the address of the property).*

[*(Or where you wish to withdraw a previous election)*

In accordance with s.799 of the Income Tax Trading and Other Income Act 2005 I hereby withdraw the election previously made that for the year ………….. *(insert the tax year for which you want the election to apply)* rent-a-room relief shall not apply to the income I received from letting …………………………………. *(insert the address of the property).*]

Yours faithfully

…………………………………. *(insert signature)*

Licence agreement (commercial property)

If you purchase a commercial property personally and then lease it to, say, your company, you could end up paying stamp duty land tax on the lease. Issuing a licence instead can avoid this potential problem.

STAMP DUTY LAND TAX - LICENCE AGREEMENT

Stamp duty land tax (SDLT) is due on the grant of a lease. The amount payable is based on the net present value (NPV), i.e. the value in today's money of all the rent payable under the lease over its full term. Where the NPV exceeds £125,000 (residential) or £150,000 (non-residential), SDLT is due at the rate of 1% of the excess.

If you let your company occupy a property owned by you personally in return for a rent, HMRC could argue that you have granted a lease, even where there is no paperwork to prove that you have done so. If it treats it as a lease, then it could seek to collect the overdue SDLT plus interest and penalties. However, this can be avoided by using a **Licence Agreement** instead of a lease. A licence cannot be sold or given away, whereas a lease can be assigned to someone else.

LICENCE AGREEMENT (COMMERCIAL PROPERTY)

In respect of .... *(insert address)*

THIS LICENCE is made on .... *(insert date)*

Between

.... *(insert name)*, ("the Licensor") and

.... *(insert Company name)*, ("the Licensee")

The Licensor and the Licensee have agreed to occupation of the premises known as ....
(insert property address) on the following terms:

The Licence to run for a term of ....*(insert term length)* commencing on ...... *(insert start date)*
and expiring on .... *(insert finish date)*. At the end of the Licence the Licensee will offer vacant
possession if a formal renewal has not been completed.

The Licence fee to be £ ..... *(insert figure)* per month, payable in advance calendar monthly by
standing order. This fee is exclusive of all non-domestic and water rates and all other outgoings
and is payable from the ....*(insert start date)*.

The Licensor reserves the right to increase or decrease the Licence fee at their discretion. The
Licensor will give the Licensee reasonable written notice of any significant increase or decrease
in the fees payable.

The Licensee to maintain and give up on termination of the Licence the interior of the premises in
as good and substantial repair and decoration as exists before this Licence commences and the
Licensee upon notice shall immediately attend to necessary repairs.

The Licensee to comply with any enactments or regulations or such like which may be required
from any competent Authority.

The Premises are not to be used other than for normal ......*(insert office/manufacturing etc.)*
purposes in connection with the Licensee's proposed business. The Licensee is not to do or
permit anything to be done on the premises which is illegal.

The Licensee to insure and keep insured the premises against loss by fire and such other perils.

The Licensee to permit the Licensor at any reasonable time to enter the premises.

The Licensee to indemnify and keep indemnified the Licensor against all actions, claims and
demands arising from the Licensee's use and occupation of the premises.

At any time within the term of the Licence, the Licensee or Licensor may give one calendar
month's notice to terminate this Licence.

By signing this agreement, the Licensee formally acknowledges that this is a Licence only and no
tenancy is created, whether formal or informal.

Signed for the Licensor: ....

Name: .... *(insert your name)*

Date: ....

Signed for the Licensee: ....

Name: .... *(insert Company name)*

Date: ....

Nominating a main residence election

If you own two or more properties which you use as homes, say your main home and an apartment by the sea you use at the weekend, you can choose which of these qualifies as your main residence for the capital gains tax private residence relief.

MORE THAN ONE

The general rule is that if you make a gain on the sale of your main residence, then you don't have to pay capital gains tax. This is called private residence relief. An unmarried individual or a married couple can only have one main residence for this relief at any one time.

However, if you have more than one home, it's possible to nominate which one you would like to be treated as your main residence.

MAKE AN ELECTION

An election can only be made where you actually live in more than one home. For example, you can't elect for a property to be your main residence if you are renting it out.

An election must be made within two years of you having two or more residences, but once an election has been made it can be switched (varied) between the properties as often as you wish. A variation can apply up to two years prior to the date you make the election. Plus, each time you acquire another property a new two-year window to make an election opens.

In the case of a married couple, both partners must sign the election for it to be effective.

You should elect to nominate the property which is likely to produce the greatest capital gain when you sell or transfer it. However, the CGT rules are generous and where an election applies for just a short time the final 18 months of ownership will also qualify for the private residence relief..

In view of the final 18-month rule, it's a good idea elect the property which you expect to make the least gain as your main residence for a short time, say a month, and then vary the election back to the original property.

You can use this document for a first time main residence election or variation.

NOMINATING A MAIN RESIDENCE ELECTION

HMRC

…………………………………..

…………………………………..

…………………………………..

………………………………….. *(insert address)*

…………………………………... *(insert date)*

………………………………….. **(insert your name)**

………………………………….. **(insert your ten-digit tax reference)**

Please accept this letter as an election to nominate ……………….. *(insert address of property)* as my [our] main residence for the purpose of principal private residence relief from Capital Gains Tax in accordance with s.222(5) of the Taxation of Chargeable Gains Act 1992.

This election is effective from ……………….. *(insert date from which it is to apply - this can be up to two years prior to the date of this letter)*. This election supersedes or varies any election I [we] have previously made.

Yours faithfully

………………………………….. *(insert signature - self)*

[………………………………….. *(insert signature - spouse)*]

Property management company contract

When companies have lower effective tax rates than individuals, it might make sense to divert some of your rental income from properties you own personally into your own property management company. In order to avoid a challenge from HMRC, there should be a formal contract between you and the company.

PROPERTY MANAGEMENT COMPANY

Whether to buy a property personally or through a limited company is a common question asked by property investors. Although companies currently have lower effective tax rates (say, 20%) than individuals (say, 40% or 45%), there could be a further tax charge when taking money out of the company as salary or dividends. However, by setting up a company to manage your property portfolio, you can take advantage of the lower company tax rates (as some or all of your rental profits will be diverted through the company). The company would provide the usual letting agent services, such as finding new tenants, ongoing maintenance, repairs and property inspections and would charge you at a commercial rate for this service. Commercial letting agents usually charge around 10% - 15% of the gross rental income for a full management service. Therefore, if you rent out a property for £1,000 a month, then the company can charge you £150 a month (15% of £1,000) as a management fee. The company could also make separate charges for drawing up a tenancy agreement or taking an inventory. To rebuff any challenges of "this is a sham" from HMRC, you should have a written **Property Management Company Contract** in place. The contract should outline the management services that the company is providing to you and their related charges.

PROPERTY MANAGEMENT COMPANY CONTRACT

Contract for management services

This agreement is made on .... *(insert date of agreement)* between

....*(insert property management company name)* (the "Company") and

.... *(insert property owner name)* (the "Property Owner")

Finding tenants

The Company will find a suitable tenant for the Property Owner for a fee of ......*(insert figure)*. This fee must be paid upon commencement of the tenancy. The service will include: continuously and vigorously advertising the property until it has been let to a suitable tenant. Interviewing and vetting all suitable prospective tenants and taking them to view the property. Taking up references from all tenants and supplying contracts.

Ongoing management service

For .... *(insert figure)* of the rental payment over the period of the Tenancy Agreement, the Company will carry out the following services on behalf of the Property Owner:

- rent collection
- notification to service companies at the commencement of the tenancy e.g. gas, electric, water, council tax
- arrangement and supervision of minor repairs to the property and general maintenance.

Additional services

Inventory

The Company will charge a fee of ....*(insert figure)* for preparing an inventory. This includes compiling an inventory for three bedrooms, two reception areas, kitchen and bedroom. For each additional room or out house there will be an extra charge of £........*(insert figure)*.

Renewal

If the original tenancy is extended for the same tenant or occupier, a further charge will become payable to the Company at the outset of such extended periods at the rate of £....*(insert figure)* of the rental payable during the extended period.

Inspections

The Company will make quarterly inspections during the period of letting to ensure the premises are being used in an appropriate manner. The charge will be £....*(insert figure)* per inspection.

Signed on behalf of the Company...

Name (in capitals) ....

Position..

Signed by the Property Owner...

Date ....

Rental business job description

You can get a tax deduction for paying your spouse/partner a wage for managing a property on your behalf. However, as with all things to do with HMRC, you have to get the paper trail right.

WAGES OF SPOUSE

As long as they don't own a share in the property, you can pay your spouse or partner a wage for dealing with the administration of your let properties. And this wage can be offset against your rental income. This is a good way for them to receive some income from the property without you having to give them a share in it. Their duties could include finding tenants, arranging inventories, check ins/outs, dealing with tenant queries, preparing the rental accounts - get your partner to sign a **Rental Business Job Description** acknowledging exactly what their duties will be.

COMMERCIAL REWARD

HMRC says you have to pay them a "proper commercial reward" for the work they do. For a commercial rate per hour, have a look at what a managing agent would charge you and then discount this by 50% for a non-specialist putting the hours in. However, you mustn't pay less than the National Minimum Wage, currently £6.50 per hour (from October 2014). It's likely that a managing agent would charge a fee of at least £15 per hour, so you could pay £7.50.

RENTAL BUSINESS JOB DESCRIPTION

Job title	Property letting administrator
Accountability	Property owner(s)
Location	Home-based and the various properties
Brief description	To run the letting business
Duties and responsibilities	1. Place adverts for tenants
	2. Arrange for inventories to be carried out
	3. Check ins/outs
	4. Dealing with tenant queries
	5. Arrange for repairs to be carried out
	6. Liaise with Gas Safe registered engineers to carry out the annual gas safety checks
	7. Keep up to date with the health and safety regulations as they apply to property landlords
	8. Carry out property inspections and updating repairs/renewals plan
	9. Rent collection
	10. Chase up overdue rent via telephone and personally
	11. Keep proper records of rental income and expenditure and prepare a monthly rental income and expenditure account
	12. Prepare the year-end rental accounts and complete the Land and Property pages of the self-assessment tax return
Hours of work	Two hours per week (flexible overtime may be required)
Transport	You are expected to use your own car to visit the properties. You will be reimbursed at the HMRC authorised mileage rates which are 45p for the first 10,000 miles and 25p thereafter
Rate of pay	£7.50 per hour

Rental income and expenditure account

To reduce the amount of rental profit, and consequently the amount of tax you pay, you need to claim as many expenses as possible. So you need a way to keep track of these expenses.

CALCULATING RENTAL PROFITS

For income tax purposes, property investment is treated as a business and, therefore, net rental income is calculated in broadly the same way as self-employed business profits. To work out your net rental profits, you need to take your gross rental income in the year and subtract any ongoing, property-related expenses. The accounting period for all rental income is the tax year, i.e. 6 April to the following 5 April .

Each tax year, you should prepare a **Rental Income and Expenditure Account** to establish whether or not you have made a profit. These accounts do not need to be submitted to HMRC - just keep them for your records and to help you complete the UK property pages on your tax return. The spreadsheet lists the various types of expense that you can deduct from your rental income. Basically, any costs that you incur in the day-to-day running of your property investment business can be deducted from your rental income. However, costs incurred in significantly improving your property are considered capital and cannot be deducted.

RENTAL INCOME AND EXPENDITURE ACCOUNT

	Apr	May	Jun	Jul	Aug	Sep	Oct	Nov	Dec	Jan	Feb	Mar	Total
Rental statement													
Rental income (excluding deposits)													
Expenses:													
Rent, rates, insurance													
Rent: Ground rent													
Service charges													
Rates: Water rates													
Council Tax paid on behalf of tenants													
Insurance: Buildings													
Contents													
Gas service contract													
Appliance cover													
Other													
Other													
Other													
Repairs, maintenance, renewals													
Repairs to property													
Repairs to fixtures and fittings													
Repairs to windows and doors													
Repairs to garden area													
Maintenance - gas													
Maintenance - electricity													
Maintenance - plumbing													
Maintenance - internal decorating													
Maintenance - external decorating													
Cost of annual gas safety certificate													

Finance charges including interest

Interest on loans to purchase property

Interest on loans to improve property for renting

Other finance charges

Legal and professional costs

Costs of agents for letting and collecting rents

Agents (etc.) charges for preparing inventories

Legal fees

Accountants' fees

Other professional costs

Services provided including wages

Gardener

Window cleaner

Cleaner

Security

Wages of those providing services for you

Cost of house clearances

Other services provided

Other services provided

Other services provided

Other expenses

Travelling (to and from property)

Stationery

Telephone calls

Other out of pocket expenses of running the business

Other expenses

Total expenses

Rental income less expenses

Wear & tear allowance

10% of gross rental income less water rates and
council tax

(Can only be claimed for fully furnished properties)

-	-	-	-	-	-	-	-	-	-	-

Net profit/loss (before tax adjustments)

-	-	-	-	-	-	-	-	-	-	-

Schedule of capital costs

Repair costs you incur on the day-to-day running of your property rental business are usually tax deductible from rental income, whereas the cost of structural alterations or improvements count as capital expenses (enhancements). These are dealt with differently for tax purposes and so it's important to keep a record of each.

ALLOCATING AND RECORDING EXPENDITURE

There may be a long gap between the time you improve or alter a property and the time you sell or transfer it. For this reason you should keep an up-to-date record of anything you spend for this purpose. You can then refer to this **Schedule of Capital Costs** when the time comes to work out your capital gains tax position following the sale or transfer of the property.

Note. Some major repair work might also count, at least partly, as an improvement or alteration making it important that you keep a record of how this expenditure is allocated between capital and day-to-day expenses for tax purposes.

SCHEDULE OF CAPITAL COSTS

Property address:...(insert address)

Date purchased:...(insert date)

Date work completed	Invoice date	Cost of work £	Amount claimed against rental income as repairs £	Amount claimed as capital enhancement costs £	Brief description of work

		Total capital expenditure added to cost of property

Wear and tear working sheet

Where an individual or company lets a residential property that is furnished, they are not entitled to claim a tax deduction for the original cost or replacement of the furnishings. They can instead claim the wear and tear allowances.

CALCULATING THE WEAR AND TEAR ALLOWANCE

The wear and tear allowance is worked out as 10% of the amount of net rents for the year or period concerned.

Net rents are calculated as the rental income received less any expenses paid by the landlord which would normally be borne by a tenant, such as water rates, heating bills or council tax.

WEAR AND TEAR WORKING SHEET

Amount of taxable rent (usually the amount received)   £

Less the following amounts paid by the landlord

    Council tax paid (except that for vacant periods)   £

    Energy bills

    Contents insurance

    Water services (rate)

Other costs normally paid by a tenant

    Total of expenses above   -

    Net rent (rent less expenses)   -

Wear and tear allowance equal to 10% of net rent   £

Section 10

Status

Checklist of status factors

Self-employed workers can be a ticking tax bomb. If HMRC decides they should have been treated as your employees, it will ask for the PAYE and NI you should have deducted from their wages plus the employers' NI due. This tax bill can cover up to four tax years (or six for NI) if the self-employed workers have been working for you throughout this period. Therefore, it's important to have documentation on file to show why you treated the workers as self-employed.

EMPLOYED OR SELF-EMPLOYED?

Ideally, you'd want all your workers to be self-employed - then you could avoid paying employers' NI, holiday and sick pay, etc. Unfortunately, you're not free to choose and HMRC is increasingly looking to challenge the status of self-employed workers and reclassify them as employed. Get it wrong and you, not the worker, will be liable for the unpaid tax and NI.

Deciding whether a worker is employed or self-employed isn't easy. And it's not helped by the fact that neither employment nor self-employment are defined in the legislation. However, there have been many cases concerning employment status and the message from these is that there are several factors to take into consideration. Our **Checklist of Status Factors** lists the most important. Fill it out as part of your procedure for taking on a new worker. Keep it as evidence to show HMRC the reasons why you treated them as self-employed. Case law shows that it is not necessary to answer "yes" to all of the questions in order to demonstrate self-employed status. You may only need one really strong indicator of self-employment to put the business into quite a safe position. Failing this, a number of weaker pointers towards self-employment coupled with the absence of any strong points against, should equally put you in a safe position. The main thing to bear in mind if ever faced by a status enquiry from HMRC is that it isn't the sole arbiter of determining employment status and its view can certainly be challenged.

CHECKLIST OF STATUS FACTORS

Worker's name and business "trading as" name if different: ....

....

NI number: ....

Checklist of status factors	Yes	No	N/A
Strong indicators:			
Would you allow the worker to provide a substitute if necessary, payment of whom will be their responsibility?			
You are not obliged to provide the worker with work e.g. during slow periods?			
Can the worker turn down work?			
Does the worker also work for other contractors?			
Does the worker provide their own tools and equipment which are fundamental to the work being carried out? (Small hand tools would be a weaker indicator.)			
Does the worker have to put right any errors or supply replacement materials at their own expense?			
No company or employee benefits are provided to the worker including paid holidays, sick pay or redundancy entitlement?			
Does the worker provide their own indemnity cover?			
Weak indicators:			
Does the contract specify that it is a contract for services?			
Is the basis of remuneration a fixed fee for work done rather than a daily rate or rate per hour?			
Does the worker have headed notepaper and invoices and bill the company for work regularly done?			
Is the worker free to work their own hours?			
Does the worker have control over how the work is done?			
Is it clear to the other company workers that the individual concerned is a contract worker and self-employed?			
Can you only terminate the agreement for a serious breach of contract?			

A "Yes" answer is indicative of self-employment while a "No" answer indicates employment.

Decision (Self-employed or employed?): ....

Made by:........................... ……………………………………………………………..

Position in company: ……………………………………………………………………..

Date: ……………………………………………………………………………………

Consultancy agreement

If you're a one-man service company, then you could be caught by IR35 if HMRC deems the contract between you and the client as one of employment rather than self-employment. Having a consultancy agreement in place can provide evidence that IR35 should not apply.

ONE-MAN SERVICE COMPANIES

Clients will often only deal with freelancers who operate through limited companies. This is because it will be the freelancer's limited company, not the client, who will be liable to any PAYE or NI (under IR35 legislation) if HMRC deems the contract between the client and the freelancer as essentially one of employment rather than self-employment.

To provide evidence to HMRC that the engagement is one of self-employment, you need a realistic **Consultancy Agreement** in place between your company and the client. The agreement should satisfy the key IR35 factors, such as the right to provide a substitute, that you do not work under the complete control of the client and that you do not expect to be provided with more work when the contract in question expires. Ensure that your working practices mirror the terms of the agreement.

CONSULTANCY AGREEMENT

THIS AGREEMENT is dated ....*(insert date)*

Between

.... ("the Client") ; and

.... ("the Supplier") *(insert your company name).*

IT IS AGREED as follows:

1. The Supplier's services

The Supplier undertakes to supply the following services: *(insert details)*

....

The terms of this Agreement will apply to all Services provided by the Supplier to the Client during the currency of this Agreement. However, the Client is not obliged to provide the Supplier with a minimum amount of work over a period of time.

2. Duration

The Agreement will be deemed to have commenced on .... *(insert date)* and will continue until completion of the Services to the reasonable satisfaction of the Client or terminated in accordance with Clause 9.

3. Performance of the services

The Supplier will be solely responsible for determining all matters of detail as to the manner in which the Services are performed, and for ensuring that all work done is of an objectively acceptable quality.

4. Independent contractor status

4.1. The Supplier is engaged as an independent contractor. Nothing herein will be deemed or construed to create a joint venture, partnership, agency or employee/employer relationship for any purpose.

4.2. The Supplier is solely responsible for payment of all taxes and NI contributions in respect of their fees and the Supplier hereby indemnifies the Client in respect of any claims that may be made by the relevant authorities against the Client in respect of income tax or NI or similar contributions relating to the Supplier's services.

5. Fee

The fee for the work shall be £ .... *(insert amount)*, which shall be exclusive of VAT (if applicable).

At the conclusion of the work (or at such intermediate stages as may be specified in the contract details), the Supplier will render an invoice for the fee on headed notepaper.

6. Provision of equipment

The Supplier will undertake the Services substantially using their own equipment and materials, the costs of which shall be deemed to have been included within the fee. Any equipment provided by the Client will be minor in scale and nature relative to this Agreement and the Client will be entitled to be reimbursed its reasonable costs of providing them.

7. Suitably qualified person

7.1. The Supplier will provide a suitably qualified person to carry out the work.

7.2. This person may be substituted by another suitably qualified person at the Supplier's expense. If the substitute does not have the necessary skills and cannot fulfil the contractual requirements then the Client reserves the right to terminate the contract.

7.3. The costs associated with any handover period will be met by the Supplier.

8. Insurance

The Supplier shall be responsible for arranging (and meeting the cost of) such insurance as they think fit in connection with this Agreement. The Client's insurance policies do not apply to any work carried out under this agreement, except to the limited extent that they would in any event protect members of the general public.

9. Obligations of the Client

Throughout the terms of this Agreement, the Client shall pay the Supplier the agreed fee in accordance with Clause 5 above.

The Client shall furnish the Supplier with sufficient information about the Services in order for the Supplier to arrange for the Services to be carried out.

The Client will advise the Supplier of any health & safety information or advice which it receives from the Client which may affect the Supplier's staff during the performance of the Services.

10. Termination

This Agreement can be terminated early by either the Client or Supplier giving three month's written notice to the other.

If the Supplier fails to perform any of the Services to the reasonable satisfaction of the Client and such failure is capable of remedy, then the Client shall instruct the Supplier to perform the work and the Supplier shall at its own cost and expense remedy such failure (and any damage resulting from such failure) within 14 days or such other period of time as the Client may direct.

In the event that the Supplier fails to comply with this clause, the Client reserves the right to terminate the Agreement by notice in writing with immediate effect.

The Supplier may terminate the contract if the Client has committed any serious or persistent breach of any of its obligations under this Agreement or in the event that the Client becomes insolvent, dissolved or subject to a winding up petition.

11. English law shall apply to this Agreement

Signed by or on behalf of the Client .... *(insert name)*

Signed by or on behalf of the Supplier .... *(insert name)*

Contract for services

HMRC's aim is to reclassify freelancers such as consultants as employees and insist that PAYE and NI is due on the total amount paid to them. Having a realistic contract for services in place will provide evidence that the engagement is one of self-employment.

CONTRACTS FOR SERVICES

Contracts for services need to be distinguished from contracts of service (i.e. of employment). Under a **Contract for Services** you can only order what is to be done, while in the case of an employee under a contract of service, not only can you say what is to be done, but also how it is to be done. One important element in a contract for services is a substitution clause. This allows the contractor to send in another suitably qualified worker in their place. Four points should be borne in mind when setting up a contract with a self-employed independent contractor:

- the right of substitution should not be limited to situations where the named worker is unable to work

- you should not be given the right to veto substitutes unless they are not suitably qualified

- you should not be able to arrange for the substitute

- the payment to the substitute must be the responsibility of the contractor and not your company.

A REALISTIC CONTRACT

Have a realistic contract between you and any freelancers you use. Ensure that your contract with them: **(1)** does not include phrases that give the impression that they are under the company's control; **(2)** gives no certainty of continuing work (this means that HMRC cannot contend what is termed "mutuality of obligation"); **(3)** includes a substitution clause; and **(4)** does not give them any employee rights such as holiday or sick pay, pension rights etc. Make sure that reality matches contract; for example, check that they are not listed in the internal telephone list of employees, and don't have the right to attend staff events (other than as an invited guest). They might even have a different security pass compared to employees.

CONTRACT FOR SERVICES

1. The Company has agreed to enter into a contract for services with *(insert name of contractor)*. This agreement will commence on the ....*(insert date)* and is scheduled to terminate on the .... *(insert date)*. Details of the work to be undertaken can be found on the attached schedule *(insert this where appropriate)*.

2. ..... *(insert name of contractor)* may offer a substitute contractor in their place, providing that all the following conditions are met:

   • the services provided by the proposed substitute remain as detailed above

   • the Company is satisfied that any substitute is suitable. In practice, this will mean that he possesses the necessary qualifications and experience to fulfil the terms of the contract

   • the Company is satisfied that the proposed substitute has sufficient resources to perform the contract to a sufficiently high standard

   • the Company is satisfied that the intended substitute will comply with its rules on confidentiality, health, safety and security

   • the costs associated with any training of the substitute and handover period will be met by ..... *(insert name of contractor)*.

   Consent to the proposed substitution is given to .... *(insert name of contractor)* in writing first.

   The Company reserves the right to refuse a proposed substitute only if the substitute does not have the necessary skills and cannot fulfil the contractual requirements.

3. ....*(insert name of contractor)* agrees that this contract does not confer an employer/employee relationship between the parties at any time.

Name ....   Name ....
(insert name of contractor) ....   *(insert name of Company representative)*

                                                        Name ....
                                                        (insert name of Company)

Signed..   Signed ....

Dated ....   Dated..

Exchange of letters

During routine compliance visits HMRC has asked companies for the names and addresses of any freelancers they use. Protect yourself with an exchange of letters between your company and the freelancer.

PROVING YOU'VE CONSIDERED STATUS

HMRC would be delighted to be able to reclassify your consultants/freelancers as your employees, as it could then insist that PAYE and NI is due on the total amount paid to them. One way to prevent this problem is to implement an **Exchange of Letters** with the freelancer on the practical aspects of their independence. This proves you both have seriously considered this assignment and genuinely regard the freelancer as independent and not an employee. Your letter and the reply from the contractor should include references to the fact that: **(1)** they have an office at home; **(2)** they bring their personal laptop computer in to the office when they do work for you; **(3)** they have a desktop computer at home that they use for their other clients; **(4)** they hold business insurance; **(5)** they have a business identity (business stationery, business cards and company-headed invoices); and **(6)** they have a business bank account through which you intend to settle their invoices.

EXCHANGE OF LETTERS

1. Letter from Company to freelancer
(For example, from ABC Software Ltd to Keith Wilson)

.... *(insert date)*

Dear .... *(insert name of freelancer, e.g. Keith)*

This letter is to confirm the points raised in the legal contract for services that both the Company and you have signed, and also deals with certain other subsidiary matters.

You have signed a contract for services, and your role with the Company from .... *(insert date, e.g. 1 October 2014)* will be as a self-employed computer consultant. Additional practical points are:

1. Your title will be .... *(insert title, e.g. independent software consultant)*.

2. Although we shall expect you to work with .... *(insert name, e.g. senior software manager, Brian Dennis)*, your relationship with them will be one of mutual co-operation, rather than your being under their management and control.

3. Your name will not be included in the internal telephone list, as you are not an employee of the Company.

4. You will be issued with a special pass for contractors and sub-contractors, enabling you to gain access to the Company's premises.

5. Although you will have access to the Company restaurant and be able to purchase lunch etc., you will not be able to use the facilities of the Company sports and health club. Attendance at any staff functions will be by invitation only as a guest.

6. Your working hours are to be agreed between you and ...... *(insert name)*. You will not be expected to "clock in" and "clock out".

7. You should present your monthly invoice to ...... *(insert name)* at the end of each month. The Company guarantees to make payment to you by the .... *(insert date)* of the following month.

8. You are not eligible for sick pay or pension contributions.

9. The Company will not pay holiday pay or bank holiday pay. Once again, it is up to you to make mutually convenient arrangements with .... *(insert name)* when you intend to be away.

10. You are responsible for payment of your own income tax and NI contributions.

11. The Company expects you to arrange your own business insurance cover.

12. When it is necessary for personnel outside the company to be contacted in connection with your work, you should make clear that you are a consultant, or arrange for an appropriate employee to deal with the matter on your behalf.

13. As set out in this contract, the Company will make payment to you for hours worked at the rate agreed.

14. When you are not available, and it is necessary for someone else to cover for you, we understand that your colleague ....*(insert name)* will substitute for you.

15. This contract is for a fixed period. If, at a later date, we would like to retain you for a further period, we will negotiate accordingly. There is no certainty that future work will be available.

We look forward to seeing you on ....*(insert date, e.g. 1 October).*

Yours sincerely

.... *(insert name)*
Director

2. Response from freelancer to Company

.... *(insert date)*

Dear .... *(insert name of a director of the company)*

Thank you for your recent letter, and I note the points raised. I would add the following:

1. I reserve the right to complete work for other clients in addition to my work for ....*(insert name of company, e.g. ABC Software Ltd).*

2. Although I shall be using .... *(insert name of Company)*'s software and hardware, I shall arrange to bring my own laptop computer into the office. I have a desktop computer at home that I use for my other clients.

3. I shall be retaining my office at home, and expect to do a certain amount of work for .... *(insert name of Company)* there.

4. I confirm that I hold public liability and other business insurance.

5. My monthly invoices will be submitted on headed paper.

6. I have business cards printed that identify me as an independent contractor.

7. I have a business bank account, and would like my fees to be paid by electronic means into this account. I will arrange for you to have the necessary account details.

I look forward to a successful and rewarding business relationship with the Company.

Yours sincerely

.... *(insert signature)*

.... *(insert name)*

IR35 calculator

IR35 potentially affects any consultant who, rather than working under a direct employment contract with a customer, contracts their services through a one-man company. If you are likely to be caught by the IR35 legislation, how much this will cost you in tax?

WHAT IS IR35?

In April 2000 a tax rule came into force (known as IR35), which potentially affects any consultant who, rather than working under a direct employment contract with a customer, contracts their services through a one-man or "personal service" company. By taking dividends rather than being paid a salary, the consultant can make substantial tax savings. The test for IR35 is whether, ignoring the existence of the company, the contract as it operates between the customer and the consultant is one which would lead to the consultant being classified as an employee of the customer, rather than self-employed. If the answer is "yes", the consultant would indeed be classified as an employee and IR35 applies. If they would be classified as self-employed, it does not. If IR35 applies, then the consultant would be required to pay tax on a "deemed" salary as if they were an employee.

Effectively, tax on 95% of turnover is charged, with a deduction only for employee-allowed expenses and professional indemnity insurance. Use our **IR35 Calculator** to work out the potential liability. **Note.** The extra tax is a liability of the consultant company and not the customer company.

IR35 CALCULATOR

Company name:

Year end :(DD/MM/YYYY)

		£	£
	Turnover to which IR35 applies		
Less:	5% automatic deduction for expenses		-
			-
Add:	Value of other payments/benefits received to which IR35 applies		
			-
Less:	**Allowable expense items**		
	Business motor expenses		
	Business travel		
	Professional subscriptions		
	Capital allowances		
	Entertaining		
	Other expenses		
	Necessary protective clothing		
	Flat rate expenses		
			-
Less:	Employer's pension payments		
	Employer's NI paid on actual pay and BIKs		
	Actual gross pay		
	Employees' NI on gross pay		
	Taxable benefits-in-kind provided		
	Total actual pay etc.		-
Less:	Deemed pay (inc Employers' NI)		-
	Employers' NI on above		-
	Deemed pay (liable to PAYE/NI)		-
Tax & NI on deemed remuneration			
	Deemed pay (see above)		-
	Personal tax-free allowance (if available)		
	Taxable income		-
	Taxable at 20% on	=	-
	Taxable at 40% on	=	-
	Taxable at 45% on	=	-
	Tax due on deemed pay		-
	Employees' NI on deemed pay		-
	Employers' NI on deemed pay		-
	Total tax and NI due on deemed pay		-

Section 11

VAT

Appeal letter

If you disagree with a VAT assessment or decision made by HMRC, you can, in most cases, appeal against it. An appeal should always be made in writing and usually within 30 days of the date of the assessment or decision.

RESOLVING DISAGREEMENTS

First step - optional. If you disagree with HMRC over a VAT assessment, a penalty imposed or a ruling or decision you can ask for an Internal Review before making a formal appeal to a tax tribunal. HMRC advises that in the first instance you should write to your local office and formally ask for an Internal Review. This is where an experienced, usually senior, officer, who wasn't previously involved in the decision you disagree with, reviews an assessment or decision. If clearly inaccurate, it will usually be withdrawn, or reduced. This review must be completed within 45 days or if you agree longer.

Second step. Where you still disagree with HMRC or want to skip the Internal Review you can appeal to the First-tier Tribunal (Tax) against the assessment or ruling in question. This should be done using the official Notice of Appeal, which can be downloaded from the gov.uk website at: https://www.gov.uk/tax-tribunal/appeal-to-tribunal.

TIME LIMIT

An appeal needs to be made within 30 days of the disputed decision by HMRC, which is normally the date of the assessment letter (if you don't want a review) or the date of the review conclusion letter. Once you have completed the Notice of Appeal form, use our **Appeal Letter** to send it to HMRC. Your professional costs will be paid if the tribunal decides that HMRC acted unreasonably in the conduct of your case.

APPEAL LETTER

First-tier Tribunal (Tax)
3rd Floor
Temple Court
35 Bull Street
Birmingham
B4 6EQ

.... *(insert date)*

.... *(insert your reference)*

Dear Sirs

.... ***(insert your business name)***

VRN .... ***(insert your VAT registration number)***

Please find enclosed a duly completed Notice of Appeal relating to the assessment made by HMRC on .... *(insert date of assessment)*.

We have enclosed a copy of the assessment for your information.

If you have any queries please do not hesitate to contact us.

Yours faithfully

.... *(insert name)*

.... *(insert company name)*

Enc

Authority letter to HMRC

If you want someone, for example your accountant or a friend, to communicate with HMRC on your behalf, you must put this in writing. If you don't, he won't be prepared to discuss your VAT or other tax affairs with anyone but you.

GETTING AROUND A CONFIDENTIALITY ISSUE

HMRC isn't allowed to reveal confidential information to a tax advisor/accountant unless it holds the authority to do so. However, although the Inland Revenue and Customs & Excise merged into Her Majesty's Revenue and Customs (HMRC), any existing authority held by the Inland Revenue doesn't work for VAT correspondence. For example, appeals to HMRC against a late filing penalty for a VAT return have been rejected because it did not hold a direct authority from the taxpayer.

HMRC has now updated its authorising your agent document (Form 64-8) to allow you to state which taxes the advisor will be dealing with, including VAT. However (pending the processing of an new 64-8 you may have submitted), we suggest sending in an **Authority Letter to HMRC** along with the next appeal/correspondence. This should avoid the hassle of the appeal being rejected or HMRC refusing to answer your advisor's letters.

AUTHORITY LETTER TO HMRC

....*(insert address)*

....

....

………………………………………. *(insert date)*

Dear Sir

I, ... *(insert name and VAT number of the trader)* authorise HMRC to disclose VAT information held about my business affairs to ……………..... *(insert name and address of nominee)* who is acting on my behalf.

This authorisation covers all VAT matters within the responsibility of HMRC and includes approaches which may be made to obtain information from all sections of the department, such as the VAT, Excise & Customs Helpline, Debt Management & Banking and the VAT Registration Service. This authority will remain in force until I give you written notice to the contrary.

Yours faithfully

.... *(signature)*

.... *(insert your name)*

.... *(insert date)*

Compensation claim letter

Chances are that sometime in your dealings with HMRC he will make an error or be responsible for a delay that costs you money. In these circumstances you can you claim compensation for this.

MAKING A COMPLAINT

Let's say HMRC comes to call and later issues you with a VAT assessment. You feel that it's wrong and obtain professional advice. The advisor agrees that the assessment is incorrect. The advisor asks for an internal review of the assessment. HMRC sees the error of its ways and withdraws the assessment in full.

However, HMRC's computer starts sending you reminders to pay the (withdrawn) assessment. HMRC has got its wires crossed and the various sections involved are not communicating with each other. This is not a matter that can be appealed to a tax tribunal, so what can you do? Write to HMRC (contact the VAT helpline on 0300 200 3700 for the address) making a formal complaint of the way the matter has been handled.

PROFESSIONAL COSTS

If you have incurred professional costs in obtaining advice on how to handle a matter, or have got your accountant/tax advisor to deal with it for you, you can ask HMRC for an ex gratia payment to cover the costs. The local office can authorise payments of up to a certain amount without referring the matter to higher authority. They are usually quite good at making these local payments, mainly because it closes the matter before it is referred to the independent Adjudicator. However, if you do not take a hard line in these matters they can run on for months and cause considerable aggravation.

Use the **Compensation Claim Letter** to claim your professional and other costs back by writing to HMRC with a detailed breakdown of these, including time taken to prepare the claim.

COMPENSATION CLAIM LETTER

HMRC

.... *(insert address)*

....

....

.... *(insert date)*

.... *(insert your reference)*

Dear Sirs

.... ***(insert your business name)***

VRN .... ***(insert your VAT registration number)***

We attach a detailed costs claim.

HMRC issued an assessment for £........ *(insert amount of assessment)* plus interest on .... *(insert date).*

.... *(insert your company name)* appealed against this assessment on .... *(insert date of your appeal letter)* which was subsequently withdrawn following negotiations.

The attached claim is for costs we incurred over the period from the date the appeal was lodged to the date it was withdrawn.

Please review the attached information and let us have your proposals for meeting out costs.

If you have any queries regarding this matter, please contact us.

Yours faithfully

.... *(insert name)*

.... *(insert company name)*

Enc

....*(insert your business name)*

VRN ....*(insert your VAT registration number)*

Details of costs claim

Charge rates:

Description	Rate	Reference
(Advisor 1)	£ X per hour	A1
(Advisor 2)	£ X per hour	A2

Calculation of costs:

Date	Description	Amount
	Telephone conversation; e-mail regarding receipt of assessment disallowing ....*(insert subject of assessment).*	A1 - 0.75 hours = £… **Total £…**
	Discussions regarding recent tax tribunal decisions regarding similar cases.	A1 - 0.25 hours = £… A2 - 0.25 hours = £… **Total £…**
	Telephone call to client. Discussions regarding background. E-mail receipt of faxed information relevant papers.	A1 - 0.5 hours = £… **Total £…**
	Research and preparation time, starting to draft reconsideration letter. E-mailing draft to client.	A1 - 2.75 hours = £… **Total £…**
	Further conversations with client, receipt of additional information by fax and e-mail regarding under-declared output VAT, preparing an internal review letter and schedule. Completion of the notice of appeal and covering letter.	A1 - 1.75 hours = £…. **Total £…**
	Receipt of HMRC letter withdrawing assessment. Letter to the tax tribunal withdrawing appeal.	A1 - 0.75 hours = £… **Total £…**
	Draft costs claim and covering letter.	A1 - 1.5 hours = £… **Total £…**
Total claim for costs		**£ X, XXX.XX**

Electronic filing checklist

If you miss the deadline for submitting your VAT return or paying your VAT electronically, you may be liable to pay a surcharge or penalty. Our checklist will help you avoid this type of trouble.

ONLINE SUBMISSION

From 1 April 2012 all businesses with a few exceptions, essentially insolvent traders and those whose religious beliefs prevent them from using computers, must submit VAT returns online and pay any VAT due electronically.

Note. With effect from 1 July 2014, businesses who are able to satisfy HMRC that it's not reasonably practicable for them to file online are also allowed to file their VAT returns on paper or by telephone.

If you miss the deadline for submitting your VAT return online or paying your VAT electronically, you may be liable to a fine. Our **Electronic Filing Checklist** will help you to file your VAT return on time.

ELECTRONIC FILING CHECKLIST

Check you have completed everything correctly	Initial
If the system won't accept your online VAT return, check that you have filled in all the relevant boxes in the correct format.	
If you do find an error, make changes to the relevant boxes and re-send it.	
Check for system errors	
If you have checked that you have completed everything corrcetly but HMRC's system still won't accept your return, check your computer's broadband connection to make sure it is working properly.	
Check with your commercial software provider, as part of your normal support arrangements, for any known glitches.	
Find out if there are any current problems with the VAT Online service by checking The "Service availability" section of HMRC's website: **http://tinyurl.com/nq8wjkq**	
Contact the VAT Online Services Helpdesk (0300 200 3701). Note time and date of your call and the advice you were given.	
If you find that you can't submit your VAT return online due to a problem with: • your own computer/broadband connection • your software provider; or • the HMRC service being unavailable then print or make a note of the error message details.	
If you see a blank page when trying to view the PDF version of your VAT return acknowledgements, this may be caused by incorrect settings within Microsoft Internet Explorer. Possible solutions to this problem can be found at: **http://tinyurl.com/33cr649**	
What if you miss the deadline?	
If, due to system problems, you think you are going to miss the deadline to submit your return online, avoid a surcharge for late payment by paying any VAT due on your return by the due date.	

360

Internal Review letter

HMRC operates a VAT internal review system to resolve disputes without the time or expenses involved with a formal appeal. If you wish to use this facility you should apply in writing to HMRC within 30 days of the assessment or decision with which you disagree.

ASKING FOR A REVIEW

If you disagree with HMRC over an assessment, you can ask for an Internal Review of the decision or you can appeal to the tax tribunal. HMRC advises that in the first instance you should write to your local office and formally ask for an Internal Review. This is where an experienced, usually senior, officer reviews an assessment or decision. If clearly inaccurate, it will usually be withdrawn, or reduced. It must complete the review within 45 days or if you agree a longer period.

If your dispute is unresolved after the Internal Review, you have the right to appeal to the tax tribunal.

INTERNAL REVIEW LETTER

HMRC

Internal Review Officer

. . . . *(insert address)*

. . . .

. . . .

. . . . *(insert date)*

. . . . *(insert your reference)*

Dear Sirs

. . . . **(insert your business name)**

VRN . . . . **(insert your VAT registration number)**

. . . . **(insert assessment number)**

We are writing to request a formal Internal Review of an .... *(insert type, e.g. assessment/decision/ruling)* dated *(..........insert date)*.

Background

. . . .
(insert details)

Grounds for review

. . . .
(insert details)

Supporting evidence is available on request.

Accordingly we would request that the assessment be withdrawn.

If you have any queries, please do not hesitate to contact us.

Yours faithfully

. . . . *(insert name)*

. . . . *(insert company name)*

Invoice checklist

From time to time HMRC makes a fuss about invoices complying with VAT regulations. And where they don't you can be fined or lose the right to reclaim VAT on purchases.

VALID VAT INVOICES

If you are registered for VAT, valid invoices are important for two main reasons:

- you can be fined if you don't issue these to your customers
- you cannot reclaim VAT on your purchases without one.

The VAT regulations set out the minimum requirement for information to be included on invoices. There are exceptions and modifications to these rules, such as the right of retailers to issue simplified documents, but most businesses must comply fully with the rules. Our checklist will help you ensure the invoices you issue and receive come up to scratch.

INVOICE CHECKLIST

An invoice you issue or receive to or from a UK-registered person should contain the following information:

1. An identifying invoice number, which must be unique and sequential

2. The date of the supply and the date when the invoice was issued

3. The name, address and VAT registration number of the supplier

4. The name and address of the customer

5. The type of supply by reference to the following categories:
   a) a supply by sale
   b) a supply on hire purchase or any similar transaction
   c) a supply by loan
   d) a supply by way of exchange
   e) a supply on hire, lease or rental
   f) a supply of goods made from customers' materials
   g) a supply by sale on commission
   h) a supply by sale or return or similar terms

6. A description sufficient to identify the goods or services supplied

7. For each description, the quantity of the goods or the extent of the services, the rate of VAT and the amount payable (excluding VAT)

8. The total amount payable (excluding VAT)

9. The rate of any cash discount offered

10. Each rate of VAT chargeable and the amount of VAT chargeable, expressed in sterling, at each such rate, and

11. The total amount of VAT chargeable, expressed in sterling.

For invoices issued to or received from a person registered in another EU country, the information required must be modified to include the following:

- the information specified at points 1 to 6 and 9 above

- the letters "GB" as a prefix to the registration number

- the registration number, if any, of the recipient of the supply of goods or services and which registration number, if any, must contain the alphabetical code of the EU country in which that recipient is registered

- the gross amount payable, excluding VAT

- where the supply is of a new means of transport (as defined in s. 95 of the VAT Act 1994) a description sufficient to identify it as such

- for each description, the quantity of the goods or the extent of the services, and where a positive rate of VAT is chargeable, the rate of VAT and the amount payable, excluding VAT, expressed in sterling, and

- where the supply of goods is a VATable supply, the information as specified at points 10 and 11 above.

Source: Regulation 14 of the VAT Regulations 1995

Letter after problems with online filing

If you've missed the deadline for submitting your VAT return online (or paying your VAT electronically), you might be let off the hook where you can show this was caused by IT problems.

EXPLAIN WHY

If you were unable to file your VAT return online because of problems with HMRC's VAT Online service, you should write to HMRC explaining why. Enclose any evidence of the steps you took.

The sort of evidence that counts in your favour includes:

- a copy of the printout of the relevant page from the HMRC website to prove what and when you were advised by its site about known problems

- a copy of the screen print/file note of the error message details showing that the HMRC site itself was unavailable

- copies of an exchange of e-mails between you and your commercial software provider about any known glitches

- and if after trying the recommendations, you continued to experience a problem and contacted HMRC's VAT Online Services helpdesk on 0300 200 3701, provide a copy of your file note showing time and date of your call and the advice you were given.

Use our **Letter After Problems with Online Filing** to help you compose your request for any surcharges etc. to be rescinded.

LETTER AFTER PROBLEMS WITH ONLINE FILING

HMRC
Local VAT office
…………………………………………….. *(insert address)*
……………………………………………..
……………………………………………..
……………………………………………..

………………………………………….. *(insert date)*

VAT number: …………………………………….

Dear Sir or Madam

Please accept this letter as explanation of why we were unable to file our electronic VAT return for the period ended ……………… *(insert period)* by the due date of ……………….. *(insert date).*Our reasons were as follows:

(Delete as appropriate)

1. We checked that all the relevant boxes on the VAT return had been filled in and with the correct format.
2. Your system still wouldn't accept our return, so we checked the HMRC website to see if there were any known problems and what to do if there were. Attached is a copy of the print out of the relevant page to prove what and when we were advised by your site.
3. The HMRC site itself was unavailable on …………………………………… *(insert times and dates)*. Attached is a copy of the screen print/file note of the error message details.
4. We checked with our commercial software provider, as part of our normal support arrangements, for any known glitches.
5. We contacted the VAT Online Services Helpdesk. Attached is a copy of our file note showing time and date of our call and the advice we were given.
6. All we saw was a blank page when trying to view the PDF version of our VAT return acknowledgements caused by incorrect settings within Microsoft Internet Explorer. This has subsequently been rectified.

Having missed the filing deadline for submitting our VAT return online (or paying our VAT electronically) we hope that we will not be liable to a surcharge for the reasons set out above.

Yours faithfully

………………………………………….. *(insert name)*

………………………………………….. *(insert position)*

Encs

Option to tax letter

Renting out land or buildings is usually exempt from VAT. This means you don't charge VAT to your tenants. The downside is that you might not be entitled to reclaim VAT on your property running expenses. By "opting to tax" the property VAT becomes payable on the rents you charge and the sale of the property. The advantage of opting to tax is that you will be allowed to claim VAT back on related purchases such as maintenance costs.

VAT ON PROPERTY

Unless you "opt to tax" a property (HMRC sometimes refers to this as "electing to waive your exemption") you must not charge VAT on any property-related supplies you make to your tenants or other persons. The option can usually be made without obtaining permission from HMRC. From the date it applies you must charge VAT on all supplies linked to the property, e.g. rents or lease premiums.

You should notify your tenant as far in advance as possible where you intend to opt to tax.

You must notify HMRC that you have opted within 30 days of it being effective. This should be done by completeing a Form VAT1614A (http://www.hmrc.gov.uk/forms/vat1614a.pdf).

Clearance from HMRC is only required where you have made exempt supplies of the property and certain conditions set out in VAT Notice 742A Section 5 are not met. In these circumstances you must ask HMRC for approval before you can opt.

The consequences of opting to tax can be complex and far reaching and we recommend getting advice from a tax advisor before going ahead. However, once the decision is made you can use our **Option to Tax Letter** to inform HMRC and enclose the completed VAT1614A.

OPTION TO TAX LETTER

HMRC
Option to Tax National Unit
Cotton House
7 Cochrane Street
Glasgow
G1 1GY

....*(insert date)*

.... *(insert your reference)*

Dear Sirs

.... ***(insert your business name)***

VRN .... ***(insert your VAT registration number if registered)***

Please accept this letter and the enclosed VAT 1614A as notification of the option to tax the land and buildings specified in the attached schedule.

We have (*not made exempt supplies related to the property/we have made exempt supplies of the property but satisfy the conditions for automatic permission to opt to tax in accordance with Notice 742A Section 5*).

The option to tax (*took/will take*) effect from …….. *(insert date)*. Please acknowledge this notification.

Yours faithfully

.... *(insert name)*

Note. A director/company secretary/sole trader, partner or trustee, whichever is applicable, should sign the notification. Failing this, another person can be authorised by written notification to sign on their behalf.

SCHEDULE

The land and buildings subject to our option to tax is located at:

……………………………………………………………………..*(insert property address)*

[We attach a plan of the land and buildings. The land registry number is……….. *(insert number)*]

Reasonable excuse letter

HMRC has a wide range of penalties available to it. Many of these can be reduced while others can be removed completely where you have a reasonable excuse for the action which gave rise to the penalty.

HAVING A REASONABLE EXCUSE

Most of the penalties imposed by HMRC will be cancelled in full if the taxpayer can establish a "reasonable excuse" defence. Unhelpfully though, there is no definition of "reasonable excuse". This argument now applies to:

- failure to notify liability; and

- default surcharge.

In relation to failure to notify liability to registration, some situations where a reasonable excuse can be established are:

- bereavement and serious illness

- unforseen events

- employment status - a person thought they were employed but were in fact self-employed

Note. The law does specify that shortage of funds and reliance on another person are not reasonable excuses for failing to notify.

With the default surcharge, there is a different list including:

- computer breakdown

- illness of key personnel

- unexpected cash crisis (but not insufficiency of funds itself); or

- loss of records.

Excuses that won't work are, for example, cheque signatories being on holiday, staff responsible for preparing VAT returns being absent due to pregnancy and the fact that there has been no significant loss of VAT.

IGNORANCE OF THE LAW

Ignorance of the law is not mentioned in HMRC's lists although it is relevant to both failure to notify and the misdeclaration penalty. For example, in one case a distinction was made between basic ignorance in relation to registering for VAT and the taxpayer's ignorance of the fact that expenses incurred abroad and charged to his customers would be regarded as part of his turnover for VAT. The issue has been raised in relation to:

- liability of particular supplies
- whether supplies are made in the course of business
- place of supply
- time of supply
- supplies involving agents or sub-contractors
- the existence of a partnership
- imports
- bad debts; and
- credit notes.

Use our **Reasonable Excuse Letter** as the base on which to build your argument that you had a reasonable excuse and so should be let off a penalty or have it reduced.

REASONABLE EXCUSE LETTER

HMRC
Internal Review Officer
....*(insert address)*
....
....

....*(insert date)*

....*(insert your reference)*

Dear Sirs

....***(insert your business name)***

VRN ....***(insert your VAT registration number)***

Reasonable Excuse for Late Submission of a VAT Return

We are writing to request a formal reconsideration of the penalty £ .... *(insert figure)* within the assessment .... *(insert assessment reference)* for £ .... *(insert amount of assessment)* plus interest issued by the Commissioners on .... *(insert date of assessment)*.

The ground for this request is that we had a reasonable excuse for the VAT return (and/or payment) for the period .... *(insert period of late return)* being submitted late. The reason for the lateness is .... *(insert details)*.

Accordingly we would request that HMRC withdraw or reduce the penalty imposed.

If you have any queries please do not hesitate to contact us.

Yours faithfully

....*(insert name)*

VAT return checklist

Making a mistake on your VAT return will result in under or overpaying VAT. This might mean losing out on VAT you can reclaim or underpaying which can result in financial penalties. Our VAT return checklist can help you reduce errors.

WHAT TO PUT ON YOUR VAT RETURN

The principle of VAT is that a business adds its output tax to its sales. If it sells to another VAT-registered business, that business may claim relief for tax it has paid on its purchases and expenses (its input tax) against its own output tax. There are also different rates for different items, and a distinction between zero-rated items and exempt items.

INPUT TAX

The basic principle of claiming input tax is that you may claim for items that can be attributed, either directly or indirectly, to the taxable supplies you make. Generally, you can claim back input tax on business items. This may seem an obvious point but you would be surprised at the number of people who try to claim back VAT on private items. Plus, certain items are specifically excluded for the purposes of claiming input tax, such as VAT on cars, entertaining, and directors' accommodation.

OUTPUT TAX

For output tax, difficulties sometimes arise in deciding what is the correct rate of tax, and what constitutes a taxable supply. Then there is a problem with cars again. If you claim input tax relief on fuel for cars, and you have any private use during the VAT period, then you must usually add a scale charge to your output VAT on your VAT return (unless you make a charge for private use of fuel when you can pay VAT on the reimbursed amount instead).

Our **VAT Return Checklist** is a box-by-box guide to what figures need to appear where on your returns.

VAT RETURN CHECKLIST

What goes on your VAT return?

Not only does VAT law change, but so do the transactions that go through your books. What's included and what's left off your online VAT return is important if you want to avoid trouble with HMRC. This is a box-by-box guide to help you get the entries right.

Box 1 - OUTPUT VAT

As well as VAT on sales and other taxable business income you should include the VAT on:

- supplies to staff (vending machines, reduced price goods etc.)
- sales of business assets and capital equipment
- motoring scale charges if you provide fuel for private use
- gifts of goods costing more than £50, excluding VAT
- the **full** value of goods sold in part-exchange
- commission received from selling other people's goods
- supplies of goods to unregistered customers in other EU member states
- self-billing invoices received
- any reverse charge services you receive (e.g. a German lawyer charges you £1,000 for work done in Germany; you charge yourself £200 (£1,000 plus 20%))
- errors in output VAT from earlier periods, but only where the net amount, i.e. taking account of any other errors on the return, is less than £10,000

Deduct the VAT on any credit notes issued.

Box 2 - EU VAT

The VAT due on any acquisitions of goods from other member states of the EU (e.g. you buy machinery from a supplier in Germany. He zero-rates the supply to you. The Sterling value of the goods is £6,000. You charge yourself VAT on the £6,000 and put it in Box 2 as your output VAT (you claim it back in Box 4 though)).

Box 3 - SUB TOTAL

Add together the totals in Boxes 1 and 2.

Box 4 - INPUT VAT

You should include:

- VAT reclaimable on purchases
- VAT on imports (taken from Customs Form C79 they send to you)
- acquisition tax accounted for in Box 2 (i.e. to cancel out the EU VAT)
- VAT on reverse charge services accounted for in Box 1
- VAT bad debt relief claims
- adjustments for credit notes received

- errors from earlier periods where the net amount is less than £10,000, i.e. taking account of any other errors on the return, is less than £10,000.

You must exclude VAT on:
- the purchase of motor cars
- business entertainment
- goods bought under one of the second-hand schemes
- purchases for personal or private use
- purchases for non-business activities
- private accommodation for directors (but not hotel accommodation when away on business).

Box 5 - NET VAT

The net amount payable/receivable (Box 3 minus Box 4).

Box 6 - NET SALES

Include the total net value of outputs including:
- standard-rated supplies (including motoring scale charges)
- zero-rated supplies
- supplies to VAT registered businesses in other EU member states
- supplies to non-VAT registered customers in other EU member states
- supplies where the place of supply is outside the UK (e.g. a UK company buys goods from Hong Kong and has them delivered directly to a customer in Australia)
- own goods transferred to another EU member state
- sales to other EU member states on a sale or return basis
- deposits for which an invoice has been issued
- exports
- exempt supplies (e.g. insurance, financial services etc.)
- reverse charge transactions.

Box 7 - NET PURCHASES

The net value of purchases including:
- imports
- EU acquisitions
- reverse charge services.

You can exclude the following from Boxes 6 and 7:
- VAT itself
- money put into or taken out of the business by you
- loans, dividends and gifts of money
- insurance claims
- stock exchange dealings
- the cost of MOT certificates
- motor vehicle licence duty
- local authority rates
- income which is outside the scope of VAT because it is not consideration for a supply, e.g. compensation.

Box 8 - EU GOODS

The total value of goods (not services) supplied to other EU member states including:

- own goods transferred to another EU member state
- supplies to VAT registered businesses in other EU member states
- supplies to non-VAT registered customers in other EU member states
- goods transferred on consignment and "call-off" stock
- sales to other EU member states on a sale or return basis
- goods dispatched from the UK for installation or assembly in another EU member state
- supplies of new means of transport
- distance sales to unregistered customers (mail order) when you are above the registration threshold in the country of destination
- costs. The values should be in Sterling and include any related costs such as commission, packing transport, insurance etc.

Note. Everything in Box 8 should also be included in Box 6.

Box 9 - EU PURCHASES

The total value of acquisitions of goods from other EU member states, including:

- any goods brought to the UK from another EU member state even if no actual purchase takes place (e.g. goods transferred between divisions of the same company)
- goods assembled or installed in the UK that have been dispatched from another EU member state.

Note. Everything in Box 9 should also appear in Box 7 of the VAT return.

Voluntary disclosure letter

If you discover an error on a previous VAT return, you will need to correct it. In most cases this can be done simply by amending your next return, but sometimes it's necessary to make a voluntary disclosure.

IF YOU FIND AN ERROR OF £10,000 OR LESS

If you discover that you've made a mistake and misdeclared the amount of VAT due, you need to adjust it. If the errors on the return add up to £10,000 or less (or, if greater, 1% of the Box 6 figure, subject to an upper limit of £50,000), you can correct these by adjusting your next VAT return. However, remember to keep a record of the adjustment and how it was calculated, so you can show HMRC next time it pays you a visit. You should record:

(1) the date the error was discovered

(2) the period in which it occurred

(3) whether it relates to input or output tax; and

(4) where the supporting documents can be found. It's a good idea to annotate the adjustment on your VAT analysis with the words "voluntary disclosure adjustment".

IF YOU FIND AN ERROR OVER £10,000

If the error is more than £10,000, you have to tell HMRC in writing. You can do this by completing a VAT Form 652 and sending it to your local VAT office. Alternatively, you could send a **Voluntary Disclosure Letter** with the details. HMRC will accept a voluntary disclosure any time before it begins "to make enquires", i.e. before it makes an appointment to inspect your records and in certain other limited circumstances.

VOLUNTARY DISCLOSURE LETTER

HMRC

.... *(insert address)*

....

....

....

.... *(insert date)*

.... *(insert your reference)*

Dear Sirs

.... ***(insert your business name)***

VRN .... ***(insert your VAT registration number)***

Voluntary disclosure

We wish to advise HMRC of an error in accounting for .... *(insert details of the error)*. We have recently been advised that .... *(insert details of the correct treatment)* and that VAT should have been accounted for on this transaction.

Accordingly, we have enclosed a schedule of ..…………. *(insert details of the error being declared)* together with the VAT due on these amounts.

If you have any queries please do not hesitate to contact us.

Yours faithfully

.... *(insert name)*

Enc

....*(insert your business name)*

VRN ....*(insert your VAT registration number)*

Voluntary Disclosure: schedule of errors

......(insert output/input) tax not accounted for on ..... *(insert the transaction).*

VAT return period	Net amount (£)	VAT (£)
Total ([under]/[over] declared)		

Written rulings letter

If you have a VAT problem, you can ring HMRC for an answer and follow its advice, but HMRC is prone to changing its mind. If the amount of VAT involved is material or the transactions affected likely to be repeated, it is a good idea to obtain a written ruling.

OBTAINING A WRITTEN RULING

If you have no evidence supporting an unusual VAT treatment you have adopted, then HMRC will assess back for up to four years to correct this "error".

HMRC now runs a VAT, Excise & Customs Helpline, that can be contacted on 0300 200 3700. The standard of advice is at best variable, but is OK for basic queries. If you need advice on anything else, ask for it in writing using the **Written Rulings Letter**. There are a number of advice centres around the country dealing with written enquiries, and you can obtain the address of your nearest one from the above mentioned helpline. Again, the standard of advice is not great, and you will normally only get HMRC's view of the law. But if you provide it with all the facts and get a written ruling, it will have to stick by it, even if the advice is wrong.

EXCUSES

It's not always that easy to get a written ruling from HMRC. Its published guidance states: *"You can write to us and ask for our view on how a particular transaction that has taken place, or is due to occur shortly, should be treated for VAT"*. However, there is a get-out clause that says it will not answer hypothetical questions. It has been known to use this excuse to dodge answering difficult questions, but if you persevere it will give you a ruling. If HMRC is initially unwilling to give a written answer, threaten it with the Adjudicator. Don't worry, we've included suitable wording in our letter to cover just such an eventuality.

WRITTEN RULINGS LETTER

(Written rulings centre obtained from National Advice Service)

....*(insert address)*

....

....

....

....*(insert date)*

....*(insert your reference)*

Dear Sirs

....***(insert your business name)***

VRN ....***(insert your VAT registration number)***

Request for written ruling

In accordance with your **Questions about VAT: writing to HMRC to get them answered** publication we are writing to ask for your view on how a particular transaction that *(has taken place or is due to occur shortly)* should be treated for VAT. This is not a hypothetical question**.**

We have considered the relevant information available on the HMRC website. In particular, we have looked at the following publications *(list the VAT notices and Business Briefs you have checked, include any paragraph numbers you consider relevant)* but we are still uncertain as to how the legislation affects the transaction set out below:

....
.... *(provide HMRC with all the facts of the transaction).*

If you are unable to give a ruling please provide a written explanation for this so I can decide whether it is appropriate to refer your refusal to the Adjudicator.

If you have any queries please do not hesitate to contact us.

Yours faithfully

....*(insert name)*

Notes

Notes

Notes

Notes

Notes

Notes